Christianity and Change

EDITED BY

NORMAN AUTTON

LONDON

S · P · C · K

1971

First published in 1971
by S.P.C.K.
Holy Trinity Church
Marylebone Road
London NW1 4DU

Made and Printed in Great Britain by
The Camelot Press Ltd, London and Southampton

SBN 281 02625 4

CONTENTS

ACKNOWLEDGEMENTS

Biblical quotations are taken from the *Revised Standard Version* of the Bible, copyrighted 1946 by the Division of Christian Education of the National Council of the Churches of Christ in the United States of America, or from the *New English Bible*, copyrighted 1961 by the Oxford and Cambridge University Presses, and are used by permission.

Thanks are due to the following for permission to quote from copyright sources:

Faber & Faber Ltd: *Period Piece: A Cambridge Childhood*, by Gwen Raverat.

Faber & Faber Ltd and Harcourt Brace Jovanovich, Inc.: *Four Quartets, Little Gidding*, by T. S. Eliot.

Macmillan & Co. Ltd and Yale University Press: *Court and the Castle*, by Rebecca West.

Oxford University Press: *Patterns of Dominance*, by Philip Mason. (Published for the Institute of Race Relations, 1970)

CONTRIBUTORS

David L. Edwards, M.A., Rector of St Margaret's, Westminster, and Canon of Westminster.

The Rt Hon. Francis Pakenham, Earl of Longford, politician and economist and holder of many important offices in successive Labour administrations.

Leslie Paul, M.A., D.C.L., F.R.S.L., formerly lecturer in Ethics and Sociology at The Queen's College, Birmingham.

Peter B. Hinchliff, PH.D., D.D., Secretary of the Missionary and Ecumenical Council of the General Synod of the Church of England.

J. S. Habgood, PH.D., Principal of The Queen's College, Birmingham, and Honorary Canon of Birmingham.

John B. Taylor, M.A., Reader in Islamic Studies, Selly Oak Colleges, Birmingham.

Douglas Webster, M.A., Canon Residentiary of St Paul's Cathedral.

Peter Baelz, M.A., Dean of Jesus College, Cambridge.

THE EDITOR, Norman Autton, M.A., D.LITT., is Director of Training of the Hospital Chaplaincies Council of the General Synod, Church House, Westminster.

Introduction

Norman Autton

What has Christianity to say to an age of bewilderment and secular thought; to an era of turmoil and terror, challenge and change? What has faith in "love almighty" to offer when confronted by the "ills unlimited" of our contemporary society? When 'foundations' shake and creeds collapse are men to find nothing but a heap of rubble, dark, despairing, dead, or in their search for meaning will they see those very stones form an Empty Tomb of light, hope, and resurrection? When in spiritual confusion and theological doubt they cry "They have taken my Lord away, and I do not know where they have laid him" (John 20.13), will a voice be heard to say "Why are you so disturbed? Why do questionings arise in your minds? Look at my hands and feet. It is I myself!" (Luke 24.39, 40). In the fog of gloom and the slough of despond along the Way, when signposts once clear now seem blurred and indistinct, will men find new grounds of hope and fresh paths of peace? In the climate of current theological thought, when processes of change are evident, will men see God in Christ actively working in these changes, offering opportunities for service and conditions for growth?

Thoughtful Christians cannot help but ask and attempt to wrestle with such questions. The chapters that follow will, it is to be hoped, further thought and stimulate discussion. They comprise a series of lectures held at Church House, Westminster, London, S.W.1., during the Autumn of 1970, and were organized by the Hospital Chaplaincies Council of the General Synod. Their theme is based on the Report of Section 1: "The Renewal of the

1

Church in Faith", in *The Lambeth Conference 1968: Resolutions and Reports* (SPCK and Seabury Press. 1968).

The opening chapter challenges the very survival of some of our basic religious beliefs in an age when Christians are having to rethink their faith; when they are being forced to search for what is true for them among the many traditions of the past. Indeed, what should a modern man believe? The next three chapters outline some of the trends of our so-called "permissive society", over which the wave of violence sweeps so frighteningly and moral standards change so drastically. We are in an age, too, when divisive factors are at work, and the need to be different seems the order of the day.

The second half of the symposium begins with an examination of the doctrine of creation and its practical implications in a world of technology. Some of the important issues involved in inter-religious dialogue are next explored, and the need stressed for confrontation in words to be matched with communion in action. Inter-religious coexistence must result in inter-religious co-operation. We are then led on to study the proclamation of the good news of the gospel in the context of a theology of mission based on man's sickness and God's salvation. In the final chapter we are brought face to face with the problems and questionings of prayer. What is prayer? Is prayer still valid? What is to be the character of Christian prayer in our secular society?

"If the trumpet call is not clear, who will prepare for battle? . . . How many different kinds of sound there are, or may be, in the world . . . How can you tell what tune is being played? . . ." (1 Cor. 14.7, 8, 10). It is only by personal and costly involvement in the human predicament of today, as it is and where it is; it is only through prayerful discussion and open dialogue with others, and a readiness to accept their criticism and benefit from it, that the Church can give a clear clarion note of hope. God through his Son, Jesus Christ, "the same yesterday, today and for ever", with whom "there is no variation, no play of passing shadows", lives and works through his creation, in the very heart of its ferment and upheaval, in its cross and in its crisis, its agony and its ecstasy. As soon as we are prepared to accept this, despair gives way to hope and faith replaces fear, for in change there will be challenge, in doubt fresh thought and in death new life.

1

The Collapse of Creed

David L. Edwards

It is a true and very important comment on our religious situation
to say that while *creed* has collapsed, *belief* has not. A "creed"
appears in a dictionary as "a professed system of religious belief,
and by extension a set of opinions on any subject". The word is
of course derived from the Latin for "I believe", but "creed"
when contrasted with "belief" is a word emphasizing both the
systematic and the opinionated character of a particular set of
beliefs. It is the receiving end of the uninhibited style of teaching
which we connect with the word "dogma". What is taught dogmatically is accepted as a creed; and that is what has been discredited.

The strongly systematic nature of "dogma" and "creed"
has been the boast of those who have taught and believed in
this style. The status of the Apostles' and Nicene Creeds in
traditional Christian theology and devotion provides a very clear
example of this. Innumerable preachers and teachers have argued
that all the clauses in those creeds stand or fall together, and
innumerable numbers of faithful worshippers have taken it for
granted that a creed must be received, and publicly recited, as a
whole, without allowing either oneself or anyone else to treat any
clause as optional. Any deviation was clearly heresy, and any idea
of revising the creed, or of discontinuing its public use, was so
arrogant as to be unthinkable for the orthodox. With great sincerity and passion, eminent Christian theologians have within
the last hundred years, as in previous ages since the time of the
Fathers, argued that belief in God could not be justified except in
connection with the belief that on the third day Jesus Christ

rose again from the dead; or that the belief that Jesus Christ was conceived of the Holy Ghost and born of the Virgin Mary (without an earthly father) was inextricably tied up with the belief in Jesus Christ as the Son of God. In European Protestantism Karl Barth and in the Church of England Charles Gore are the greatest theological names one recalls in this connection, but the same teaching has been heard from many thousands of Protestant or Anglican pulpits, and of course the Roman Catholic and Eastern Orthodox Churches have steadily taken it for granted.

Moreover, the right of some teaching authority to propound a creed has been believed in as that creed's invisible and inaudible first clause. Conceptions of doctrinal authority have, of course, differed, and some of the controversies arising have been fierce and epoch-making. Some Christians have held that the creed can be proved from the Bible because the Bible either constitutes or contains the Word of God. Other Christians have obeyed the teaching of the Church because the Church, or its Pope, or its hierarchy, or the best section of its theologians, has been held to be divinely inspired. But all these Christians have agreed that there is such a thing as truth revealed by God and stated in propositions which should never be either contradicted or changed. The task of theology is, on this showing, not adventure but commentary; and the duty of the individual is not to test but to obey. The reverence surrounding the creed has expressed the humility of faith.

The formulation of Christian belief in an ancient creed has commanded such obedience, even during the twentieth century, because it has seemed to provide a rock-like authority amid the ebb and flow of human opinions. The feeling among religiously minded people that a firm authority was psychologically necessary has been widespread, and for many this feeling has only been increased by the revolutionary and chaotic violence of the storm which has raged in the intellectual ocean. We can all recall dramatic and moving examples of the submission of an individual to a doctrinal system when there has seemed to be no other possible foundation for that individual's security or sanity. The examples which we easily recall are no doubt extreme, but essentially the same attitude has been shared by many who have endorsed a traditional creed, or who have found it necessary to pretend to others or even to themselves that they have endorsed it; and I suppose that almost everyone shares this feeling to some extent, because almost everyone feels some humility towards the past. In addition to this phenomenon of reaction against religious doubt or confusion there have also been instances, even in the twentieth century, of a perfectly calm and well-reasoned conclusion that the creed happens to be in every respect true. There have also been examples of an acceptance of religious authority without the consideration of any alternative; examples of a theological innocence. It would be wrong to suppose that creeds have usually been imposed by an ecclesiastical police, although certainly the Vatican and some Protestant authorities have applied frightening pressure on waverers. What has counted for most has been the wish of countless Christians, with varied motives, to preserve a creed because through that they have found joy and peace in believing.

I hope that I have now said enough to remind you of the outline of the theological scene as it has been known to our forefathers and to many of us, and as it still comes alive whenever a worshipper gets up in church and, together with everyone else in the congregation, recites a formula many centuries old after the introductory words "I believe . . .". I hope too that I need not spend much time in describing the process by which this theological scene, familiar to so many generations, has gradually been eroded like a beautiful coastline being eaten away by a stormy sea. For this process is surely within the experience of many of us.

A great shock has come from the fact, only slowly and painfully discovered but now incontestable, that the Bible contains errors. Some of these errors are historical inaccuracies, but others are matters of opinion, and one thinks them wrong only if one sets one opinion in the Bible alongside another, seeing the Bible not as one document of uniform verbal authority, but as a library reflecting beliefs held by very different people in very different situations over more than a thousand years. The result of modern critical study of the Bible has been to show that the contents of this historically conditioned library must be judged as to their religious value in the light of beliefs held for some reason other than that "the Bible tells me so". Many Christians have thought this all along, and have found the desired authority outside the Bible in the Church, whose tradition has been believed to be sacred and in carefully defined places to be infallible. But it has become increasingly difficult to think that the Church is infallible. Most unfortunately, the Popes have taught *ex cathedra* doctrines about the character and end of the life of the Virgin Mary in history for which there is no good historical evidence. The proclamation by Pope Pius XII of the physical Assumption of Mary seems to be the only Papal act since 1870 which must be regarded as infallible according to the criteria of the First Vatican Council which then defined Papal infallibility, but of course the teaching authority of the modern Popes has been helped neither by their prohibition of artificial birth control nor by their equivocation in the face of the Nazi extermination of the Jews, for the limitation of the world's exploding population and the crusade against the evils of racial hatred seem to most thoughtful people today to be among the most urgent moral issues confronting mankind, and the conscience of mankind would declare that on both these issues the Papacy has got itself in a tragically wrong position. And in the background the frequent hesitations or outright hostility of the ecclesiastical authorities around the world under the challenge of scientific discoveries and social progress may fairly be regarded as a factor in the decline of the Church's reputation. It is not hard to see why the idea of the infallible Church seems to be undergoing the same fate as the idea of the inerrant Bible—among thoughtful Roman Catholics as elsewhere.

It would have been pleasant to say that the ancient and hallowed symbol of the Christian faith, the Apostles' Creed, had emerged unscathed from modern criticism of the Bible and the Church. It has, indeed, been generally regarded as far less objectionable than the so-called "Athanasian" Creed, which makes the scandalous claim that those who do not accept its doctrines about the Trinity will without doubt perish everlastingly. And of course the so-called "Apostles'" Creed is shorter than the so-called "Nicene" Creed, and less tied to outmoded philosophical terms such as "substance" in describing the incarnation of the Son of God. But it so happens that the Roman baptismal creed traditionally associated with the Apostles, when examined about eighteen hundred years after its first use, is found to include phrases which most people, whether or not they wish to be regarded as Christians, do not take literally. Many modern Christians who accept and recite this creed do so with their own interpretation based on their own experience and thought, thus damaging the simple, unquestionable authority which the plain words and obvious meanings of this creed possessed in the old days. Although so venerable, the Apostles' Creed, the crown of the whole structure which was built on the old foundations, has not remained absolutely unmoved while the foundations have been shaken.

You will forgive me if I do not spend long in discharging the thankless duty of echoing modern criticism of the use of the Apostles' Creed in a world so different from that when it was compiled. Some of these criticisms have questioned the simple old description of God as "Almighty", because of the notorious prominence of evil, and suggestions have been made that "Sovereign" would be a less misleading adjective to apply to the power which God exercises. That is a philosophical objection. I have already hinted at the difficulties which most modern people experience in the doctrines of the virginal conception and physical resurrection of Jesus; difficulties which may be called historical. Other modern reactions to the Apostles' Creed are insistent that some of its language is mythological, specifically the clauses about the descent into hell (or the place of departed spirits) and about the session on the right hand of the Father. Modern people do not readily understand such myths, and it is also true to say that they do not easily picture the end of human life on this planet as consisting of the return of Jesus from God's right hand, or the eternal hope as consisting of the resurrection of the body (or of the flesh, as it is put in versions of the Apostles' Creed which accurately reflect the original Latin). Some honest modern reactions to the Creed would be confessions of puzzlement about what is meant by statements such as "I believe in God . . . Maker of Heaven and Earth" or "I believe in the Holy Catholick Church" (many libraries have been written in controversies there); and some modern reactions would be complaints about what is left out. We may suppose that no one trying to express the faith of twentieth-century Christians would put a mere comma between the birth and arrest of Jesus, as the Apostles' Creed does; for it is only the personality of Jesus, as shown in his teachings, his healings of the sick, and his dealings with his followers, that ever persuades modern minds that thinking out what is true in the ancient creeds is worth the effort.

I have now come to the end of the destructive part of my case. What I want to say now is that I utterly reject an argument which has often been advanced after this kind of analysis of the difficulties in theology: the argument that no kind of religious belief is worthy of respect in the age when our view of the world around us and of the history behind us is, or ought to be, scientific. On the contrary, I think that religious belief does and should continue during the age of science. The only difference is that it must now assume a form different from its shape during the long centuries when, in creeds, systems of dogmas were taught confidently and accepted wholeheartedly.

What kind of religious belief can survive? One approach to that question has recently received what almost amounts to an official blessing in Anglican circles. The Archbishops' Commission on Christian Doctrine and the 1968 Lambeth Conference of Bishops have both published reports which indicate the general approach of emphasizing the varied richness of our theological heritage instead of this or that particular clause in a traditional "standard of belief". The conclusion of this line of thought would seem to be that the ancient creeds, while retained in use, need to be balanced with each other, with the Bible, with the theology of every significant Christian group and period, and with the modern individual's reason and conscience. A Christian's loyalty is to the whole of this tradition, but not necessarily to any one fragment of it. If I may say so, this seems to me an approach which, if generally followed, will enable long-hallowed formulae such as the creeds to be used as symbols of a general assent to Christianity, and will at the same time liberate Church leaders and theologians from the shackles of the past. But it does not go far enough in answering the inquirer's nagging question: *Is it true? Is it true for me?*

I think that in the period into which we are moving it is inevitable that we should pick and choose among all the treasures and the junk which we have inherited from nineteen centuries of Christianity. Unless we are to split our personalities into half which is Christian and half which is modern—and I am sorry to say that a policy very like that is often recommended to us by leaders who ought to know better—we cannot swallow the Bible whole, or the Church whole, or even the more diffused Christian tradition whole. And, if we must in conscience be courteously selective among those ancient glories, how much more necessary is discrimination in our attitude to more recent and more obviously passing theological systems! For better or for worse, there simply is not available in the world today a religious system which deserves our complete loyalty. In a way this is our burden. On the whole people have been happier than we are when they have been able to take their basic beliefs and values for granted; when they have felt secure and at home, and when they have been able to devote their energies to the task of living according to some generally accepted laws. We glimpse this happiness today in simple tribal or rural societies, or in well-integrated members of closely knit communities such as regiments or research teams, or in some fundamentalists, whether Protestants or Catholics. But most of us are for most of the time involved in a pluralist situation: that is, we know that the real world around us is too complicated, and that we ourselves are too complicated, to fit into any of the grand old simplifications. And for us, to opt out of that situation would be to opt out of reality.

If we are to pick and choose, what standards do we use to guide our choice? There seems to be only one real criterion, once the unreality of creeds has been acknowledged. I have never found a better way of expressing this than by quoting some words of Paul Tillich, the words which I put in the front of *The Honest to God Debate* when I edited that book seven long but not very productive years ago.

> The words which are most used in religion are also those whose genuine meaning is almost completely lost and whose impact on the human mind is nearly negligible. . . . There is only one way to re-establish their original meaning and power; namely, to ask ourselves what these words mean for our lives; to ask whether or not they are able to communicate something infinitely important to us.

That is, I see an existentialist approach as the only valid way for modern men into the ancient mysteries of religion. Literally everything in the tradition, however venerable or however repulsive, must be passed through the single test: *Do I believe this as a result of my own experience?*

Take, for example, the beliefs behind the Apostles' Creed. The acknowledgement of God's power, and of the origin of all things in God's creativity, must spring out of men's experience of God in daily life, not out of pseudo-scientific speculation. The conviction that the life of Jesus Christ on earth came out of God's love for the world, and not only out of Joseph's love for Mary, must result from how we have felt the continuing impact of Jesus Christ, not from pseudo-historical research. The faith that the crucified is in deepest reality crowned, and as the risen Lord is the best pattern to show the goal of human evolution, must come to birth not as we read the books of theologians but as we think for ourselves, so to speak, at the foot of the cross of Jesus Christ, and as we walk along our own road, so to speak, on the way to Emmaus. Belief in God the active Spirit, or belief in the distinctive and universal mission of the Christian fellowship, or belief in human destiny as being more than death, must similarly arise not from what our teachers tell us but from what we learn through our own often agonized puzzlement, through the intuitions which come to us, through our own deep reliance on others (specially on our fellow-Christians), and on our own wonder as we put the fact of our spirituality beside the prospect of our graves. Human life is the soil where human belief is rooted. Christian experience is where Christian faith grows.

Belief of that kind, rooted in real existence, is in some ways unsatisfactory. It does not give us the authority to pontificate about what happened at the dawn of time, or at the first Christmas or Easter. It does not provide us with a comprehensive assessment of all that is known or should be known. It does not enable us to lay down the law to others. If we thus base our beliefs, we shall be agnostics in reply to many questions metaphysical, scientific, or ethical. "I don't know" will be a phrase often on our lips and—worse still!—often in our hearts. But we know what matters to us, because we know what we have learned in our own mysterious existence. Above all, we know the real, living, and eternal Master whom we have met for ourselves, and whom we have tried to follow along a path which is known only to us and, we now believe, to him; and through that encounter with Jesus Christ we know the real, living, and eternal God. One of the latest documents in the New Testament provides a charter for Christian existentialism in these words: *I know who it is in whom I have trusted* (2 Tim. 1.12, NEB). If such roots are strong, dead leaves of the tree may safely be allowed to fall.

You will have noticed that the variety of Christian existentialism which I have thus briefly presented is not of the very austere type which confines authentic Christianity to the disciple's relationship with the Master without drawing any conclusions about the reality of God or (to mention a comparatively trivial subject) the necessity of the Church. I am not trying to say that loyalty to Jesus is compatible with the conviction that God is dead. I am simply repeating what innumerable Christians have found: that Jesus is the true and living way into God, God's world, God's Church, and God's victory. I am not even implying that every use of every creed in Christian worship and teaching is illegitimate. On the contrary, I take it for granted that treasures so sacred as the Apostles' and Nicene Creeds will never be lost, and that every thoughtful Christian to the end of time will come to terms with them as with St Paul's letters or St John's Gospel. In church services it seems right to use the creeds as we use the Psalms or *Te Deum Laudamus,* or the other great hymns of Christendom: in order to remind us that we worship as members of a Church which has worshipped the same God through the same Christ in the power of the same Spirit in many times and places. That is why I am able to conduct worship according to the Book of Common Prayer, and am proud and happy to do so. I am also open to the prospect of securing ecumenical agreement one day for a new creed of Christendom. All I am wanting to say is that the ancient creeds should not be given too much emphasis in Christian thought or worship at the expense of modern experience, knowledge, and thought. All I am wanting to remember is that, in the last analysis, I *believe*—or I do not. All I am wanting to stress is what I see when, amid the ceremony of a great act of worship in Westminster Abbey, I sit in the sacrarium and I contemplate the Ten Commandments upheld by Moses on the screen behind the high altar. Moses holds up as the fourth commandment what is the essence of Christian existentialism: *Remember that thou* . . . (full stop!)

You will have noticed, too, that I have not divorced the existentialist approach from metaphysical, historical, scientific, or ethical questions. Some existentialists have done that, or have seemed to do that, and they have rightly been accused of reducing religion to self-consciousness. On the contrary, I am sure that a human being, to be fully human, must turn from contemplating himself to thinking about his fellow men, about nature and history, and about his own duty in the urgent battles of life. But I have admitted the limitation of what we can know to what we have experienced, apart from what can be deduced analytically according to the laws of logic or what can be verified by scientific and historical research. The price seems fair enough, if I can have my own answer to any of the basic age-old religious problems, arising out of my own experience which has suggested my own belief as I stand in this baffling universe. It is worth my while to live amid many doubts and errors if I can use to cover my life the words which a Frenchman recently used as the title of a book: *God Exists, I have Met Him*; or, to mention a far more solid book, it does not matter if there has to be a large element of agnosticism in true theology, provided that it can venture on its tasks with the success that attended Professor John Macquarrie in his book on *The Principles of Christian Theology* (1966).

Am I alone in seeking such a sure foundation for my belief? Obviously not. All over the Christian world people are now rethinking their faith, asking themselves what is true for them in the tradition they have received, responding to theologians of the integrity and range of Professor Macquarrie, but expressing their own convictions in their own words. Ours is a time when the Churches are in disarray, their institutions in decline, their dogmas in confusion; but it is also a time of great heart-searching and even vitality. So often I have met churchgoers who go to church in spite of every discouragement because they have found something real and indispensable in the life of the Church. So often too I have met people on the fringes of the Churches who wrestle with these questions in complete seriousness and sincerity. The most memorable days of the existentialist movement—the days when against a background of Europe in flames the austere philosophy of Heidegger or Sartre seemed a deliverance from an otherwise overwhelming anxiety—are over now. The pioneering has gone and the mistakes of the pioneers are being forgotten. But the movement has profoundly influenced the whole world of thought, and particularly the world of religious thought, where we are all existentialists now.

And beyond those people who identify themselves as religious or interested in religion, I see or hear about many millions of people who are also keenly interested in the question, what a modern man should believe. Without getting sentimental about the younger generation, we can surely say that the younger generation is not coldly metaphysical, or backward-looking, or interested only in the precise questions which the natural sciences can answer, or indifferent to the feelings and sufferings of others, or lacking in a moral passion (however selective), or content with a crudely materialist view of human destiny, or uninterested in a religious vision of life. Too many of the books which describe the modern outlook were written before the protest of youth at the cruel triviality of modern life made itself heard; they were written more than five years ago. If we need a new phrase, we can say now that we are moving into a post-modern and post-scientific age. We, and even more our successors, are going to go on, not backwards. We are never going to return to the womb of a cosy creed within a neatly ordered nursery of a world. Nor are we going to return to the anxieties which coloured the expression of existentialism in the 1940s. We turn to the future in determination and even confidence. But we are certainly never going to be content with any interpretation of human existence which excludes questions of belief. Who am I? What parts or aspects of me matter most? What am I to do here? What help will be given to me? What will I find at the end of the road? These are the great human questions, asked in the 1970s with as much insistence as ever before. This is an age when an answer out of one's experience, addressed to such questions, will not be rejected merely because it involves looking beyond one's nose into the world of values which is opened by belief.

As I see it, the spiritual crisis of the 1970s is caused by the inadequacy of the answers to these questions given in the world-wide culture of youth, pop, and protest, coupled with the reluctance of people whose wisdom is more mature to move out of positions in which good answers have become fossilized and therefore irrelevant. I do not think that "love" as expounded in today's songs is going to provide a permanently satisfying answer to these questions, as the beautiful young animals grow up and have to face all life's realities. Even less do I think that the temporary physical thrills of sex and drugs are going to provide a permanently satisfying means of escape from spiritual failure. But on the basis of our experience so far there seems to me no reasonable ground for hoping that the creeds of the old religious institutions will communicate "something infinitely important" to many members of the oncoming generations. The analogy between that kind of religion and the corruption of Marxism is too alarmingly close. Conservative Christians often notice how disastrous to honest thought Communist censorship can be; how stultifying can be the bureaucratic curb on enterprise; how dangerous is the blind loyalty to the Party of some converts; and how rigid is the dogmatism which controls official Communist propaganda. Christians often regret that the creativity of Marx and Lenin has not been matched by their successors, who have relied instead on physical or emotional blackmail. And Christians have often laughed at the mutual insults and the civil wars in the Communist camp, as each side has accused the other of deviationism or revisionism. But this corruption of Marxism is no laughing matter. Communism's general failure to move into better times and to adopt a "human face" is one of those major tragedies which have so far thoroughly blighted the high promise of the twentieth century. And many Christians are not really entitled to weep for the fate of Marxism; for their own monolithic interpretation of Christianity, enforced where possible by a totalitarian Church, comes perilously close at point after point. Just as Marxism needs a "human face" if there is to be social progress, so Christianity needs a new face, a less dogmatic face, if the spiritual progress of mankind is not to be halted. A combination of Christianity and Marxism, each with a new face of human freedom, would rise to the challenge put to the custodians of the ancestral wisdom by the generation which is now coming into its own. That would save our children from the spiritual suicide which, as everyone agrees, would result from a technological revolution without a heart. And I see no alternative except the arrival of an adequately successful new religion—and there are no signs of that on the horizon that I have noticed.

The question whether *belief* must always involve a systematic, dogmatic *creed* is therefore not an academic question, but is a question for all who want man to have a spiritual future.

2

The Permissive Society

Lord Longford

There is not, as far as I am aware, any authoritative definition of a permissive society, or of a trend towards a permissive society. At this moment of time, October 1970, someone who was asked what first came into their head when "the permissive society" was mentioned, might refer to the sexual farce *Oh! Calcutta!*, or to obscenity in public entertainment generally. I will mention *Oh! Calcutta!* later. With this essay in mind, I felt it my duty to pay a visit there, strictly as a sociologist, and was, incidentally, at least as much bored as disgusted.

Some time ago the *Evening Standard*, commenting on "the latest poll on permissiveness", expressed the view: "A majority of people in Britain are now 'permissive'—if the criterion is acceptance of extra-marital sex." As a matter of fact, the polls in question did not reveal precisely this. The public were asked about the availability of the Pill for unmarried girls, and about the right course for an unmarried girl to follow if and when she becomes pregnant. They were not asked the straightforward question: "Do you think extra-marital sex is permissible?"

The last time I was involved in a debate on that question was at the Oxford Union some years ago, when we, the old fuddy-duddy Christians, prevailed by two to one. I will touch on this question later, but I do not believe that anyone is in the position to say at the moment whether the majority of the public, old or young, do, or do not, favour extra-marital fornication.

However, I would prefer to start with a quotation from Mr James Callaghan, Home Secretary at the time, who was speaking on 27 January 1969, on cannabis and the report of the Government Committee, of which Lady Wootton was Chairman. "I think", said Mr Callaghan, "that it came as a surprise, if not a shock, to most people when that notorious advertisement appeared in *The Times,* in 1967, to find that there is a lobby in favour of legalizing cannabis." (Incidentally, the Wootton Report did not favour legalizing cannabis, but reducing the penalties.) "The existence of this lobby", said Mr Callaghan, "is something that the House and public opinion should take into account and be ready to combat, as I am. It is another aspect of the so-called 'permissive society'." So spoke Mr Callaghan in January 1969. He was glad that his decision against the Report had enabled the House to call a halt in the advancing tide of so-called permissiveness. "I regard it as one of the most unlikeable words that has been invented in recent years. If only we would regard ourselves as a compassionate society, an unselfish society, or a responsible society, I would feel prouder of 1969. This conclusion", he went on, "is another aspect of the same thing and I was encouraged by the overwhelming response in the House of Commons to the statement I made last Thursday"— that was the statement in which he turned down the Wootton Report.

It would seem from what was said by Mr Callaghan, and also by Mr Hogg, now Lord Hailsham, from the other side of the House, that the phrase "permissive society", if not exactly a dirty word, is one which politicians today are very chary of applying to their own policies. Mr Roy Jenkins, who has been to the fore in many of the developments associated in the public mind with permissiveness, prefers to speak of "the civilized society". Mr Wilson, like Mr Callaghan, refers to "the compassionate society". I pick out leaders from what is sometimes called "the progressive side" of politics, although the issues that we are now considering cut somewhat across party lines. Nevertheless, few observers would deny that a number of trends have revealed themselves in recent years (the same, of course, is true of other countries, but I am speaking of England), which can be perhaps more profitably discussed under the heading of "permissiveness" than of any other available term.

What do I mean by a permissive society, or a trend towards a permissive society? I distinguish, initially, three concepts: the first involves a relaxation of the criminal law in its relation to moral conduct; the second involves a relaxation of moral standards; the third involves a more compassionate attitude to those who break the law (for example, by housebreaking) or who offend existing conventions (for example, by running off with someone else's wife). If one wishes to be more meticulous, one might distinguish a fourth, somewhere between the first and the second: a relaxation of social pressures on those who relax their moral standards. For example: a parent today may not wish to invoke criminal sanctions against pre-marital fornication, nor believe such relationships to be morally right, and yet be less ready than of old to condemn a child who indulges in them.

The first and second concepts and the additional one just mentioned, as we shall see in a moment, are separate, but very hard to keep apart. The third can be handled much more easily on its own.

Any of us is at liberty to place the start of the modern trend of permissiveness where he chooses. Personally, I find a turning-point in the publication of the Wolfenden Report in 1957, more particularly in its conclusion that homosexual conduct between consulting adults should be no longer a criminal offence. A decade later that reform, as we are all aware, passed on to the statute book through the initiative of Lord Arran, Mr Abse, and many others. When the Wolfenden Report first appeared, however, the House of Commons didn't dare debate it until a year had passed. At the end of 1957 I myself initiated a debate on it, in which I indicated my clear support for the proposal in question. I believe that I was called by Lord Boothby "the non-playing Captain of the homosexual team", but I certainly did not venture to test the issue by a vote in the Lords at that time. I called the Wolfenden Report a turning-point, not so much because of the particular recommendations on homosexualism or anything else, but because of the principle which it laid down, and on which it based its individual conclusions. May I quote the key passage from the Wolfenden Report of 1957:

The function of the criminal law, in so far as it concerns the subject of this Inquiry, is to preserve public order and decency, to protect the citizen from what is offensive and injurious, and to provide sufficient safeguards against exploitation and corruption of others, particularly those who are specially vulnerable because they are young, weak in body or in mind, inexperienced, or in a state of special physical, official or economic dependence. It is not, in our view, the function of the law to intervene in the private lives of citizens, or to seek to enforce any particular pattern of behaviour further than is necessary to carry out the purposes we have outlined.

I ventured to simplify the point of view of the Committee in these words of my own: "If someone is doing wrong, the law must not intervene to stop him or her, unless they are harming someone else." Rather to my surprise, reading through my speech the other day, I find that I accepted this general principle with fewer reservations than I would make now, although I continue to applaud the particular reform about consenting adults.

In 1957 I went on to ask: "Can we accept this doctrine, that is to say, the doctrine that the law must not intervene to stop some-one who is doing wrong, unless he or she is harming someone else? By and large", I said, "though it is for each Member of the House to decide for himself, I think we can." I gave a reason in words, which as far as they go, I would not try to improve today. I said that I was not arguing that it would be morally wrong for the State to intervene in all cases to protect people from them-selves, or their friendly associates. I was arguing that, from long experience, it had been found as a general rule that that could not be done without interfering with private life and human liberty so drastically as to undermine the whole growth of moral responsibility.

What has been the agreed contention behind the ten years of successful agitation for the removal of the criminal sanction on homosexual conduct between consenting adults? Basically, it has been the argument that I have just set out. It has not been, at any rate on the face of it, a new argument about the morality or immorality of homosexualism as such. That is still condemned by society as a whole as sinful, or immoral, or antisocial, or whatever words one likes to use. It is probably not quite so much condemned as it was, in view of our greater understanding of its causes and, at this point, it is rather difficult to keep away from my third heading, a greater leniency towards offenders. I notice that I ended my 1957 speech with an adaptation of some words from Ruskin: "Let us be merciful while we still have mercy." Basically, however, I would submit that the major change in the last ten or twelve years in this field has not been due to acceptance of homosexualism as such. It has been due far more to increasing acceptance of the Wolfenden principle that the law must not step in merely to prevent grown-up people from hurting themselves.

It is instructive perhaps to glance at the abortion law reform, which was passed into law in 1967, and made legal abortions, to say the least, vastly more available. If autobiography can be forgiven again, I was the first to advocate the Wolfenden reform in either House of Parliament, but I was so strongly opposed to the Abortion Law Reform that I left my seat on the front bench, as Leader of the House of Lords, to speak against it from the back benches. (It was like the other reforms I am discussing, a Private Member's Bill.)

I am not concerned here with the merits or demerits of abortion; I am simply using it to illustrate various aspects of the concept of permissiveness. On the face of it, one could argue that it stood on the same footing as the Wolfenden amendment. All legal reforms after all (this one like the rest) are concerned with changing the law. In the nature of things they cannot directly by statute alter morals. But I would venture to point out two distinctions between the Abortion and the Homosexual Bills.

An act of abortion does after all involve someone else in addition to the woman who secures it. There is the unborn child or, as it can technically be called, the foetus. I realize that those who support abortion wholeheartedly do not pay a great deal of attention to this consideration. However, the logical distinction is there. Again, the movement to legalize many kinds of abortions was a movement that was aimed, by a high proportion of its champions, not just at altering the criminal law, but at altering our whole attitude to abortion, at persuading us to recognize that abortion was far more often the right thing to do than society had previously admitted. (I will leave out illegal abortions as complicating the issue.)

When the nation altered the law about homosexualism, they were not being asked to say that homosexualism between consenting adults was morally all right after all, but that is exactly what they were asked to say about abortion under a wide variety of conditions, and they gave an affirmative answer. In this case, very much more clearly than in the homosexual one, the change in the criminal law was intended to indicate our carrying further a change in moral conduct.

Look for a moment, and for purposes of symmetry, at the Divorce Law Reform which became law in 1969. Divorce Law Reform is not, of course, something new in the last fifteen years. I was election agent for Mr A. P. Herbert in 1935 in the Oxford University Election. Divorce Law Reform was perhaps the most striking feature of his programme and certainly the Act that followed his election facilitated divorce immensely. Some years after 1935 I became a Roman Catholic. I look forward with some apprehension to extra years in purgatory on account of my 1935 activities, but, as I have written elsewhere in tribute to Sir Alan Herbert on his eightieth birthday, I expect to scrape through in the end, if I stick close enough to Alan Herbert's heels!

What perhaps was most striking in the Act of 1969 was the provision that enabled a guilty party to obtain a divorce after a separation of five years in the shortest case. Strictly speaking, the Wolfenden principle would not be sufficient here to prevail on its own. Suppose X leaves his wife Y and lives for five years with Z and then wishes to divorce Y. It is clear that X and Z are not just like two consenting adults who, in theory at any rate, have no one else to consider. They are in fact likely to be damaging Y, the first wife, very seriously.

I ventured to say to the House of Lords: "I acknowledge that in a few cases these provisions for getting rid of an unwanted wife after a few years may, on balance, increase rather than diminish the total happiness. But I would say, with absolute conviction, that in the vast majority of cases these provisions will have a very cruel impact and for that reason I am totally against this Bill."

In general, the supporters of the Bill took their stand on an argument from Liberty and an argument from Suffering. They certainly would claim to be moved by both ideas or emotions. They also had, of course, the additional advantage of being able to point out what nonsense the existing law had become. Whatever may be said, however, about Divorce Reform as a whole, I cannot believe that the provision I have just referred to, that is, the right of the guilty partner to get shot of the innocent one after five years, would ever have been accepted by the nation if the argument had been confined to the balance of suffering. I feel sure that it was the product of a more libertarian age in which we are much less inclined than hitherto to stop people doing what they want to do in the moral sphere. So here again, the change in the criminal law and the change in moral attitudes, both as cause and effect of the legal change, are fairly well mixed up.

I suppose that I should add that the Bishops in the House of Lords were divided. I never myself accept the crude statement that there has been in recent years a clearly evident decline in religion, but I would agree that religious values are challenged more openly than of old and religious leaders have become much more uncertain how far they should try to impose a code of morals on those who do not accept their religious premises.

I must here make a brief reference to euthanasia. When the Divorce Reform Law was going through the House of Lords, I predicted that euthanasia would be soon before us. In fact, there was a Bill for Voluntary Euthanasia brought before the House of Lords in March 1969. It was defeated by 61 to 40—not a very convincing majority. Since then, the House of Commons appears to be strongly opposed to it, so there may be something of a breathing space. But I think the same kind of ideas which led to the Abortion Bill and some at least of the same ardent champions will be much in evidence in the near future on behalf of euthanasia. The medical profession at the moment seems very hostile, but I believe that the philosophical defences have yet to be worked out, unless we are to rely, as of course Christians are entitled to rely, on a Christian view of the sacredness of human life.

I now pick up the question of obscenity in public, but I will be fairly restrained and brief. When we are told that we are developing a more civilized society, and the reforms in the obscenity laws and the abolition of the Lord Chamberlain are taken as examples, we are, I think, being given a double message. On the one hand, we are here, as in other fields I have been discussing, accepting a modern idea of non-interference. At one of the earlier Pop Festivals, surprise was expressed when a young girl danced about stark naked. There would be less surprise now. "Let her alone," said her companions, "she is only doing her thing." One aspect certainly of the permissive society, or if you prefer, the civilized society, is a greater toleration. Today it is widely assumed that if I, a rather puritanical Roman Catholic, hear that a pornographic show is being put on, either in a strip-tease establishment or a public theatre, there is no reason what-ever why I should seek to interfere, or try to persuade the police to interfere. Why shouldn't they do their thing?

The argument becomes rather entangled in view of modern methods of advertisement and still more when we reach television. We are a long way here from consenting adults misbehaving themselves in private. There is the argument from toleration, and it is reinforced by a widespread view that artistic values have a standing of their own which puts them, so to speak, on an equal footing with moral values. When there is a clash, or appearance of a clash, between them, there is no reason (we are told) why artistic values should give way. Indeed, the powerful lobby, not altogether organized, of artists and communicators everywhere instinctively spring forward to argue that there must be some clearly demonstrable damage to society before the art, or alleged art, should be interfered with. The artists, including for this purpose all who wield the pen in public, or appear professionally on television, are clearly going to take a lot of stopping, although it is not clear (to me at least) that the majority of the nation sides with them. The simple fact is that it is almost impossible to prove or argue very convincingly that one particular show corrupts or tends to corrupt anyone. I have no doubt whatever that if a young person went regularly to shows like *Oh! Calcutta!* he would be damaged, but as the law stands, the dice are loaded on the side of performances which I, and many others, regard as monstrously improper.

That, however, was by way of parenthesis. Where does Britain stand officially in regard to the permissive society in so far as we agree on what that must be presumed to mean? I think that many people who read Mr Callaghan's slapping-down of the Wootton Report would be inclined to think of that report as a classic illustration of the up-to-date permissive point of view. In fact, Lady Wootton and her colleagues were much more guarded in their statement of what I have called "the general Wolfenden philosophy" (which goes far outside homosexualism) than the Wolfenden Committee themselves. They refer to what they call the controversial question whether, and if so how far, it is justi-fiable for the law to restrict a man's freedom in what is presumed to be his own interest. On that issue, they say that there is considerable support today for J. S. Mill's dictum that "the only purpose for which power can rightly be exercised over any member of a civilized community against his will is to prevent harm to others. His own good, either physical or moral, is not a sufficient warrant." They quote the Wolfenden Committee in support of this principle. But they go on to qualify that principle with carefully pondered words:

> While we appreciate the force of this argument, it has to be recognized that no hard and fast line can be drawn between actions that are purely self-regarding and those that involve wider social consequences. If, generally speaking, everyone is entitled to decide for himself what he will eat, drink, or smoke, the fact remains that those who indulge in gross intemperance of almost any kind will nearly always become a burden to their families, the public authorities or both. Indeed, examples of actions which never in any circumstances involve social repercussions are by no means easy to find. Nor can it be said that any consistent principle dictates the occasions on which the law at present intervenes to protect the individual from himself.

Every proposal to restrict the freedom of the individual in his own supposed interests must, therefore, be decided on merit, in the light of the probable severity of any damage that he may inflict upon himself, and of the risk that in damaging himself he may also involuntarily be the cause of injury to others.

On the face of it there is nothing here which Mr Callaghan and Mr Hogg, or I myself might object to. Yet I feel that there is a difference of emphasis between the very expert and high-minded people who produced the Wootton Report on cannabis and the best minds in the House of Commons today. It is not, I hope, unfair to treat the discussion in the Wootton Report of the alleged progression from cannabis to, for example, heroin addiction as much more exiguous and flimsy than one would have wished. I refer you to paragraphs 47–51 of the Report. In paragraph 51 we are told that a number of isolated studies have been published none of which demonstrate significant lines of progression. "Our witnesses [says the Report] had nothing to add to the information already available and we have concluded that a risk of progression to heroin from cannabis is not a reason for retaining the control over this drug." In other words there is no real discernible evidence, or what social scientists call evidence, that any connection exists between cannabis and heroin.

On the other hand, speaking more generally (that is, of the cannabis issue as a whole), Mr Hogg asserted: "One would think that the burden of proof lay on the people who wanted to prevent the adoption of a new vice. . . . I submit that the burden of proof lies on those who wish to go soft on soft drugs and not on those who wish to remain tough on them." Mr Callaghan in effect agreed with him and, if I may say so, so do I. The question of the burden of proof is, in my opinion, of the highest significance in all these discussions. The truth is that nothing is ever proved in a truly scientific way in the social sciences and, if we are going to say that you must not interfere with self-destruction unless you can prove scientifically that you have good reasons for doing so, you will never interfere at all.

Let us at this point call attention to a whole wide area of discussion which we have not embarked on and which involves the question of how far, if at all, the relaxing of the criminal law leads on inevitably to a relaxation of moral standards, more adultery, more pre-marital fornication and all the rest. Here, as elsewhere, we must not expect too much of social science, real or alleged. Let us conduct all the research in the world, but at the end don't let us persuade ourselves that the issues are going to be settled for us by coercive statistics. In the end, we shall all have to make up our own minds about the values themselves, and about the kind of discussions and the kind of actions and provisions that are likely to affect them.

I personally believe that changes in the criminal law will always have an important indirect effect on morals. But the public arguments surrounding the proposed changes and the atmosphere resulting from the discussion will have much *more* effect. It is high time that those who have their own clear views on Christian morals should bestir themselves more actively than hitherto. They should equip themselves, if necessary at very considerable labour, for strenuous debates in the market place. In those debates the Christian or orthodox moralist will always be listened to most earnestly if he can speak from first-hand experience of helping people in need, irrespective of their class or opinions.

But he must not expect total victory or total defeat in this striving but imperfect world. He must expect the battle line of moral and social argument to sway this way and that, into the indefinite future.

Finally, I come to what I call the third concept in the permissive philosophy, to what is, I hope, a more compassionate approach to delinquents and other deviationists. Certainly, compared with a hundred years ago, we have made immense progress. It is a far cry from the 1830s when, for example, two homosexual offenders were hanged on a separate platform, so as not to contaminate the ordinary murderers! The examples of penal progress since those days are endless.

Whether we have made much progress since the war is much more open to question. We have abolished hanging; that at least is a large and, I believe, a permanent achievement. No one supposes that murder is regarded as any less of a crime than it was, but for a lot of reasons, including some advances in psychology, we are much less brutal to the murderer. Yet even here we have a long way to go before we provide anything like a humane prospect for those convicted of murder. I speak as one who is in friendly contact with several who are serving life sentences for this crime.

Many who know a great deal about penal reform can be heard to say that the official measures taken in the name of security after the Mountbatten Report have put back the clock for quite a few years. The coming of parole is, it is true, a great advance; but even so, there are four times as many people in prison as there were before the war, hundreds of them living two, or even three, in a cell. So offenders are not getting off so very lightly. There is no doubt that prisoners who have been in and out of prison for many years will say that the system today is somewhat more humane than it used to be. But compared with advances in technology and, for that matter, in the other social services, the present system can still be described as last in the queue.

The first immediate explanation is the shortage of resources, human and material, which are allocated to the treatment of delinquents. That fact itself is a clear commentary on the extent of our collective compassion. In a negative sense, we are no doubt less ready than we were to tolerate physical maltreatment of prisoners by flogging, for example, as a punishment. On the positive side, we have not yet been prepared, as a nation, to make the relatively small financial sacrifices required to produce a reasonable level of prison buildings or, still more important, of prison officers and probation and after-care officers. But in addition to this parsimony, though partly perhaps responsible for it, lies a deeper philosophic uncertainty about our communal approach to the delinquent.

In finishing I propose to make one or two quotations from the Gospels, which have a close bearing on our subject. In the 18th chapter of St Matthew, our Lord dealt in the same passage with our treatment of children and of moral delinquents:

> Never despise one of these little ones; I tell you, they have their guardian angels in heaven, who look continually on the face of my heavenly Father. What do you think? Suppose a man has a hundred sheep. If one of them strays, does he not leave the other ninety-nine on the hillside and go in search of the one that strayed? And if he should find it, I tell you this: he is more delighted over that sheep than over the ninety-nine that never strayed. In the same way, it is not your heavenly Father's will that one of these little ones should be lost.

And in the same vein, in Luke 5 he teaches:

> It is not the healthy that need a doctor, but the sick; I have not come to invite virtuous people, but to call sinners to repentance.

From one point of view at least, the children, the sick, and the sinners are all placed on the same footing, and combined in their claim on us by their overwhelming need.

In Matthew 25, the first half of the famous passage about the sheep and the goats begins: "For when I was hungry, you gave me food . . ." and finishes, "when in prison, you visited me". All this is straightforward enough and points to a Christian duty which is clear enough to everyone, Christian or non Christian, who cares for his fellow-man.

But that is only one part of the story. Our Lord said to the woman taken in adultery, "Neither do I condemn thee"—but he said, just as emphatically, "Go and *sin no more*". Throughout the Gospels our Lord never fails for a moment to emphasize his love for us and our duty to love one another. He equally never neglects the fact of our sinfulness or allows us to neglect it. The Christian must labour unceasingly to draw his practical approach to the delinquent from the time-honoured slogan, "hate the sin and love the sinner". Old-fashioned Christians find it easy enough to hate the sins of others, but far harder to love the sinner. Progressives, Christian and Humanist alike, find it easy if not to love the sinner, at least to avoid condemning him. They shrink from hating, or at least denouncing sin, unless it takes one or two social or political forms which happen to affront them.

It is not until we proclaim, and live, the double doctrine—the denunciation of the sin indeed as part of our love for the sinner —that we shall secure the active assent of the community as a whole. And not until then shall we bring about the national dedication, financial, intellectual, and spiritual, which alone will make it possible to call our society compassionate in deed as well as word.

3

The Vogue of Violence

Leslie Paul

I grew up in one of the most peaceful periods in British history and one most free from crime. In the London of my boyhood and youth it was safe to go anywhere and walk anywhere, and I walked hundreds of miles in and around London. It was safe too on open spaces at night. I never heard of boy or girl or old lady being molested or assaulted and in my teens I was a youth leader and heard everything from my many followers. Indeed I might say that night walks in the city and on leafy deserted roads were one of my delights.

But about ten years ago a boy was kicked to death by other youths on a Thames towing-path near Putney. It was literally "for kicks", for they did not know their victim, and had no quarrel with him. He was simply a chance quarry on whom they could expend their lust for violence. In the same year a little girl I knew was hunted down in Battersea Park by teenage boys on bicycles. She fell and was badly grazed on her face and knees. Some of the boys were even known, but the mother was afraid of complaining to the police in case the boys took revenge on the little girl. Some time ago some youngsters at Wimbledon (including girls) hunted down a supposed homosexual and beat him to death with sticks. In 1968 a man was stabbed to death by a youth in the road outside the chapel at The Queen's College in Birmingham, at night. As I understand the story the boys had been on a day trip to Paris, bought flick-knives there, were high on amphetamine, and broke. They were prospecting cars for money or things to steal. When the owner of a car tried to stop them, a youth turned and stabbed him. I recall that when, some thirteen years before, a case of stabbing of a youth came before a coroner, he gravely expressed the opinion that it must have been the work of foreigners, since stabbing was almost unknown in England. Apart from records of razor slashing between race gangs, I believe he was right.

The rise in crimes of violence in England and Wales in post-war years, indeed in the last two decades especially, was spelt out for everybody to read in a series of articles by Norman Fowler in *The Times* in April 1970. He showed that for murder and atempted murder there had been an increase of 26 per cent between 1955 and 1965, and yet another 26 per cent increase between 1965 and 1968. For felonious woundings the percentage increases are: 1965 over 1955, 109; 1968 over 1965, 9: for rape, over the same years, 82 per cent and 34 per cent: for robbery (which is theft of property accompanied by force or the threat of force), 354 per cent and 34 per cent. Indeed, for all selected major crimes the two percentages are 297 and 19.[1] The curves on the graph show England and Wales as increasingly violent as well as increasingly criminal. It is not a pretty picture for a society once the most law-abiding in the world.

Of course, the plague of violence has always been worse in the United States. One must speak of America as the violent society. In many American cities it is not safe to walk the streets at night or to drive with the driving seat window down. The tabloids are full of pictures of recently stabbed or shot-down victims. I won't bother you with the statistics which show the United States at the top of the league for personal crimes of violence, but serious observers are not only alarmed by the rising curve of the crime graph but by two other things: the deliberate cult of protest violence (Black Power, student revolution, and so on) and the growth of public indifference or callousness towards acts of violence.

Kitty Genovese, only 28, was trailed by a man in Kew Gardens, Queens, New York, in March 1964, when I myself was in the United States. He attacked and slew her. At least forty persons heard her scream and shout for help, and many of them must have seen her die. No one came to her aid or called the police. One witness, asked why he did nothing, said, "I didn't want to get involved." Later the same year at least thirty persons ignored the cries for help of a Bronx telephone girl attacked by a rapist. Fortunately two patrolmen heard in time to go to her aid and

[1] *The Times,* 7 April 1970.

save her life. I myself have tried to give publicity to the following incident.[1] In Toledo, Ohio, in 1965 a truck-driver citizen was honoured because, among many pieces of conspicuous bravery in the course of his life, he rushed over to an overturned car which had caught fire and rescued the trapped woman driver. "Whadda yer want to do that for?" one bystander asked, plainly regarding the rescuer as a spoilsport.

But if one wants to get a close look at American violence one must read *In Cold Blood* by Truman Capote. It is a human and psychological study of two murderers who brutally, senselessly wiped out an entire family they had never met before and against whom they could have had no grudge. Not as rapists or robbers, or out of blood lust, but for the same kind of kicks that made those youths slay a stranger on the Putney towpath. Yet Capote's book is not only an exciting if claustrophobic narrative of this evil enterprise: it symbolizes the American fascination for the killers that Capote's identification with Smith and Hickock is almost complete, while his interest in the victims, the Clutter family, is by comparison, to say the least, marginal. This chills and frightens me. Of course, the personality and punishment of murderers is of enormous social interest. But in a curious way and by identification they can become the heroic figures of the Bonnie and Clyde kind of legend. Yet society cannot begin to heal its violence until there is compassionate identification with the victims rather than the murderers. This happens spontaneously if they are children and young people. The middle-aged and old are often viewed as though they somehow wanted or invited the violence that slew them.

That I am not inventing or misjudging is established by the justification of murder which appears from time to time. I expect you know Norman Mailer's *An American Dream*. The theme of this book, which I regard as wholly meretricious in a literary sense, is Rojack's murder of his wife, which she is shown fully to "deserve", and how he gets away with it. Of course Mailer was challenged about a book which seemed to justify murder, and he replied with great candour "I don't think anyone ever condemns murder *really*. Society may be founded on Kant's categorical imperative, but individual murder gives a sense of life to those around the event. Take newspaper readers—doesn't

[1] In *The Death and Resurrection of the Church* (Hodder 1968), p. 122.

the suburban commuter get a moment of pleasure on the subway reading about murder? Is he perverse or is it really something life-giving? I prefer the second view of man, the less bleak one." Later in the same interview (with David Leitch of the *Sunday Times*) he said, "I don't know about the social consequences: all I know is that a man feels good when he commits a murder— immediately after, that is. Have you ever seen soldiers coming back from a killing spree? They're happy. If I wrote any other way about it, it would be meretricious." These empty-headed and cold-blooded remarks typify a certain contemporary irresponsibility about murder and violence. The mandate they hand out to the vicious, the malicious, the immature, the unbalanced, the psychotic was brought home to Mailer in the hardest way. John and Robert Kennedy were his friends. There is no record of Mailer appearing in defence of their slayers.

Mailer's is not an isolated voice. I have myself many times drawn attention to the works of Jean Genet and William Burroughs.[1] Both these writers, I would argue, celebrate perversion and murder to a degree that any civilization acknowledging humanist or Christian roots ought to find both extraordinary and horrifying. Yet I find myself absolutely alone in this protest.

Genet writes, in *Our Lady of the Flowers*, among other things, and not with any irony, "To love a murderer, to love to commit a crime in cahoots with the young half-breed pictured on the cover of the torn book. I want to sing murder, for I love murderers, to sing it plainly. Without pretending for example that I want to be redeemed through it, though I do yearn for redemption. I would like to kill. As I have said above, rather than an old man, I would like to kill a handsome blond boy. . . ." (Even Genet's dedication of his book is to a murderer.)

And this is the writer—undoubtedly a great writer—who has been canonized by Jean Paul-Sartre. Saint Genet! This means accepted into the canon of the sacred literature of the high culture of European civilization and presently to be a subject in university courses in French literature and at High School. As I have said, these are not solitary instances. For they follow indeed the canonization of the Marquis de Sade whose works are everywhere read and are in paperback. The Hindley-Brady duo of the Moors

[1] *Inter alia*, in *Alternatives to Christian Belief* (Hodder 1967), Chapter 9; in *Coming to Terms with Sex* (Collins 1969), Chapter 12.

murders had resort privately to the works of the Marquis de Sade
in justification of their murders and Brady pressed his view on the
young David Smith he hoped to make his disciple. The attack
upon ethical principles accepted by Western civilization since time
immemorial, though conducted among an intelligentsia which
does not expect itself to be murdered, is not in fact without consequences at the level of concrete events.

There has been, however, a justification of violence at a different
ideological level altogether in recent years. The de Sade-Mailer-
Genet formula is that murder is an act of self-fulfilment which is
life-giving for the murderer, a deed on a par with the orgasm
which often accompanies the act. They are thinking of its personal
psychological importance, of murder as a creative act (if you can
stomach this supreme perversion). But in the student unrest and
the revolutionary guerilla ideology the moral justification of
violence has been the famous "thought" of Mao Tse-tung—
"power flows out of the barrel of a rifle". In other words that
violence is the legitimate answer of the revolutionary to the
society he opposes.

This is not a dogma which can easily be dismissed. It is bound
up with theories of the State propagated relentlessly by the
theoretical and practical revolutionaries of the last two centuries.
It really is the argument that State power is illegitimate *in toto*.
One classical Marxist doctrine has always been that all State
power is oppressive. The State is argued to be the political
instrument which a ruling class forges to keep itself in power and
to defend its properties and privileges against the classes under-
neath it which it exploits and which are the source of its wealth.
As Jean Jaurès once said (though he said it of the dictatorship of
the proletariat) the State power is a band of brigands camping on
society—and plundering it. This kind of doctrine singles out the
oppressive instruments of a State—armies, police, courts, jails—
and labels them the principal instruments of power, but links
them with the "ruling ideology" which the ruling class seeks to
impose on servile masses through religion, schools, universities,
mass media, propaganda, bribes, and rewards. It is a black and
white picture—a total arbitrary and illegitimate State power on
the one side and a totally deprived, exploited, deceived society on
the other. You can only be on the one side or the other. There is
no middle way. One is either a dumb (in the American sense)

instrument of oppression or a revolutionary fighter. It is the fantastic mystique of Tariq Ali or Che Guevara and can always be argued to be "proved" by the massive injustices of contemporary society and by the retaliation the stance itself automatically provokes. It is worth comment that, since successful revolutions become tyrannies in their turn, the only possible position for an honest man is to be a permanent revolutionary. This was the attitude adopted by Tariq Ali, I believe, and could well have been Che Guevara's, had he lived. It is not possible to exempt Herbert Marcuse from responsibility for the spread of this view. And the shape of contemporary society, particularly the growth of massive anonymous power structures—source so often of secret and irreversible social decisions, a growth I myself have tried to expose—makes it easier to adopt the position that one ought to be opposed to every established social structure because it is an instrument of the detested ruling power.

But contemporary society is not built out of black and white squares like kitchen tiling. Is a school an oppressive instrument? Many a schoolboy subject to its violent punishment has thought so. Or is it the bearer of the treasures of a culture opened out for the willing pupil to plunder? Emlyn Williams must have thought this of his village school under its devoted head. Many of us are under the same kind of debt. Is a university one or the other? Earlier generations of students saw universities as torchbearers: some of the present generation seek their destruction as the State in little. Those who fall for it are driven by the logic of this revolutionary stance not just to opposing the State but to hatred of society, or at least all parts of it they dislike, and so to justifying everything and anything which is against society, irrespective of its morality or utility. This way is nihilism.

Norman Mailer sums up this identification: "Well, it seems to me there are two kinds of violence, and they are altogether different. One is personal violence—an act of violence by man or woman, against other men or women. The second kind is social violence—concentration camps, nuclear warfare. If one wants to carry the notion far enough, there are subtler forms of social violence such as censorship, or excessively organized piety, or charity drives."[1]

[1] Norman Mailer, "Talking of Violence" in *Violence in the Streets*, ed. Shalom Endleman. Duckworth 1969.

And in the same interview he reveals the significant link between the high intelligentsia's theme of violence (murder) as an act of self-fulfilment and the ideological justification of violence as a necessary part of the war against the State (or society). "Threatened with the extinction of our possibilities, we react with chronic rage. Violence begins, you see, as the desire to fight one's way out of a trap. Moral questions over the nature of one's violence come only as a secondary matter. The first re-actions, the heart of the violence, is the protection of the self. The second question, the moral question, is whether the self deserves to be protected, that is to say—was it honourable to fight? Was the danger true? For example, if a boy beats up an old woman, he may be protecting himself by discharging a rage which would destroy his body if it were left to work it out on the cells, so he takes it out on the old woman."

Well, perhaps that is not as straightforward a link as I thought at first reading, though Mailer does go on to speak of Hemingway, and of how men who have lived a great deal with violence are usually gentler and more tolerant than, for instance, their social opposite, the university trained intellectual. But in his ambiguous answers to his interviewer the point is there, of violence as some sort of answer, right or wrong, to personal or social suffocation. Yet there is an uncomfortable slanting. It is impossible to think of him using his illustration the other way round—of an old woman preserving her body cells by beating up a boy, of an older Brady possibly justified in murdering the little girl, Lesley Downey, because he was suffocated in some sort of trap! But Mailer is interesting and important because he does straddle both camps—the high cultural joy in extreme violence and the serious ideological defence of it from militant action groups, such as the anti-Vietnam-war demonstrations he participated in and so faithfully reported.

As significant also in the straddling of the gap is the whole movement of student protest. I have spoken at some length about the political ideology of the Sorbonne and the L.S.E., Columbia and Berkeley. But the student revolt is not just political, but cultural: a youth culture, strident, aggressive, even obscene is fostered to shock the old and sever the young from them, to assert in fact the most absolute break with the past. It owes much to the hippy demands for complete sexual freedom and freedom to take pot or other drugs the young people have a mind to. A writer in the (student) Los Angeles Free Press[1] wrote: "Dope smoking clearly shows the space between the generations. It distinguishes 'young from old'. It is the most obvious sign, for those who need one, of the Revolution. Dope smoking continues, increases, while the law, broken so casually, is reduced to horseshit." The same violence of idea and obscenity of language, the same linkage of sex, dope, and violence is to be found in this quotation from *RAT* which Stephen Spender also uses.[2] "What difference can there be between shoving liberty up the ass of Vietnam and giving America love in the same way? (When you're up against a wall the gun may loom larger than the man and a penis without human context loses the power of creation.)"

In pop festivals or student revolts young people sleep together and copulate in public view. To care about this would be to share adult hypocrisies. As one poet, quoted by Spender, writes, "Plus je fais l'amour plus je fais la révolution, plus je fais la révolution plus je fais l'amour. Luttez dans la perspective d'une vie passionante." But that is elegant language compared with the forced brutality of the underground writing.

Violence receives the same kind of reassessment. Violence is the honourable, necessary thing and resort to it is the proof of one's sincerity and commitment, particularly since the old and the bourgeois disapprove of all violence except their own. Hence the spectacle of Columbia University students rushing round to find what aggressive act to do next, whether occupying a building or kidnapping a president, which would compel the authorities to reveal what an oppressive lot they were.

I want to leave the literary and ideological scene and speak of some social aspects of violence. One aspect is undoubtedly the correlation between urbanization and violence. Assuming that we all have the same intrinsic propensity for violence—in that we all share the same Freudian frustrations or experience Mailer's rages at suffocation—we do not, as it happens, resort to violence in the same degree. John Paul Scott seeks to show in "The Anatomy of Violence" in *Violence in the Streets*, that the incidence of violence

---

[1] Quoted by Stephen Spender in *The Year of the Young Rebels* (Weidenfeld and Nicolson 1969), p. 8.

[2] Op. cit., p. 6.

is correlated with the size of a city. Cities show an aggravated assault rate twice as great as the rates for suburban and rural areas, while cities of over 250,000 population show a rate four times greater than that of rural areas. Robbery and forcible rape follow similar patterns "with an almost perfect correlation between city size and crime rate".

But there are other correlations too. Deprived groups in society show inevitably higher crime rates than other groups. As we might expect, negro groups in American society show a higher homicide rate than white groups; indeed the difference is startling. "Although Negroes comprise only approximately 10·5% of total population, 2,154, i.e. 60% of all city arrests for murder and non-negligent manslaughter in 1961 were negroes and only 1,493 were white."[1] It also appears true that the worse the social deprivation of the negro (i.e. in the South) the higher the homicide rate. And this kind of analysis can be applied to all sorts of social groups to show that the more severe the relative deprivation of the group the higher its crime rate, including especially acts of violence. It makes Mailer's point, perhaps, that the deeper the social hopelessness, the higher the rage potential and readiness to strike out, if not to strike back. In one sense this is a hopeful argument. If indeed violence is correlated with social conditions then it should be possible, if the right conditions can be found, not only to reduce the violence of individuals but to reduce the violence between nations, ever a utopian hope. But in another sense it is an alarming argument. If violence is correlated with social deprivation and if that sense of deprivation is made greater and more compelling by the anonymity and humiliation of crowded, complex, rundown city areas, then the probability is that violence will increase as cities grow (and grow faster than their parts can be renewed) in the population explosion which seems upon us.

Is that all there is to be said about it? If so, we should all instantly become social determinists and strive for the ideal social situations which would remove the viper's sting of violence. But one author I have quoted spoke of American sects as recruited from deprived people—in the lowest income groups in the population—but at

[1] Dr Lewis A. Coser, "Violence and the Social Structure", in *Violence in the Streets*, p. 73.

the same time showing one of the lowest crime rates. This was because, he thought, they had removed themselves into a climate in which they did not feel their social deprivation. They no longer made the envious comparisons others made. I am sure though that they felt the lack of good shoes for their feet—and yet did not steal them! They had moved into a *moral* climate where certain acts were morally intolerable, as well as incompatible with membership of the group. The campaign against working-class drunkenness in the last century in industrial Britain succeeded not because deprivation ended but because drunkenness came to be seen as morally intolerable as well as socially hurtful.

I make this point because, however good we may be as psychologists, ideologists, or sociologists there is still a great moral battle to be fought in the minds of modern men over the sacredness of the human person; his right to the peaceful pursuit of his avocation; his right to freedom of speech, movement, and conscience; his right to freedom from terror, oppression, bodily violence, and so on. These are natural law rights, humanist rights, Christian rights. But unless men are prepared to preach them and defend them they will be lost. They are already the great casualty of this century, a century which I once described as *The Age of Terror*.

It is an urgent matter, for our civilization is already slipping back into a darker age, despite its technological momentum (some might say, because of it). For this reason I conclude with this quotation from Rebecca West's *Court and the Castle*:

Hamlet was so far from being incapable of action that he committed without remorse that extreme action, murder, and he committed it four times and killed a man in self-defence. It is sometimes said that the violence of Shakespeare's age accounts for many of the crimes in his plays. But there is surely a constant way of regarding murder, as we ourselves should know. Of all people who are elderly today it is true that when they studied Shakespeare at school they were looking back at an age more barbarous than their own, and that when they read him in later life they were looking back at an age more civilized than their own, for though the Tudors were bloodstained they were not stained with as much blood as modern dictators. Yet at no time during the recent degeneration of history would an artist engaged on a pure work of art not involved in propaganda or a person engaged in a disinterested study of a pure work of art, have considered murder as other than a horrible deed. There is built into our flesh a strong prejudice in favour of natural death.

Alas, the prejudice does not seem to inhabit all *literary* flesh. But then Rebecca West was writing long, long ago. In 1957 in fact, which puts her with the old and square of a vanished age.

FOR FURTHER READING

U.S. National Commission on the Causes and Prevention of Violence, 1968–9. Federal Government Printing Office, Washington, D.C.

TED GURR, *Why Men Rebel: a Theoretical Analysis of Political Violence*. Princetown U.P. 1969.

H. L. NIEBURG, *Political Violence: the Behavioural Process*. St Martin's Press, New York, 1969.

TRUMAN CAPOTE, *In Cold Blood*. 1966.

STEPHEN SPENDER, *The Year of the Young Rebels*. 1969.

Violence in the Streets: an Analysis of the Destructive Impulses of Society, a symposium edited by Shalom Endleman. 1969.

KONRAD LORENZ, *On Aggression*. 1967.

LESLIE PAUL, *Coming to Terms with Sex*. 1969.

GORDON RATTRAY TAYLOR, *The Doomsday Book*. 1970.

4

The Stress of Disunity

Peter B. Hinchliff

I must make it clear at the outset that I shall not concern myself particularly with Christian or ecclesiastical disunity, but with human disunity in general—though, my job being what it is, I can hardly ignore Christian disunity altogether. But the thing that interests me most is that disunity should be included at all in the list of half-a-dozen most obvious and most alarming of human ills. It is obvious and alarming to us. I doubt whether it would have seemed so to most previous generations.

I do not doubt that there has always been disunity—nor that it has always been a bad thing. What I am suggesting is that we are far more conscious of its existence and of its unpleasantness. In the third century A.D. St Cyprian wrote a depressing account of what was wrong with his world.[1] It is a pretty comprehensive list of wrongs (he is, for example, convinced that the weather is not what it was in his young days!) but human disunity does not loom large, in spite of the fact that Christian unity was one of the things that Cyprian worried about most. In the sixth century Cassiodorus was one of those who tried to introduce the principles of administration, inherited from Rome, into the government of the barbarian kingdoms. In describing what he believed to be the chief functions of administration[2] he does not deal with the need to preserve a unified society, in spite of the fact that for men such as him the break-up of the old Europe was an obvious catastrophe. The Middle Ages took universalism for granted and Dante believed that the Holy Roman Empire was bringing peace

[1] *Ad Demetrianum.*   [2] Cassiodorus, *Variae*, XI, viii.

39

and unity to Europe. Disunity was certainly an evil, but it was not high on the list of those things which made the lot of fallen human beings so uncomfortable. Machiavelli, with a new grasp of the essential principles of politics as the art of the possible, seemed to think that one achieved national unity by playing upon human *dis*unity.

One might go on for a long time making further lists like this one. Of course it is true that one can compile another list of people who believed that, if human unity was destroyed, chaos must inevitably reign. Paul and Augustine would be at one end of the list, John Richard Green and Karl Marx at the other. What confuses the issue is that they did not always think this would be a bad thing. But, on the whole, most men have assumed that unity is good, that we must not lose it, that we must look to preserve and improve it. The emotive language that Christian theologians have used about heresy and schism, the very terms themselves that imply the ripping and slashing and dragging apart, convey this fear and hatred of what might be round the corner—chaos, disruption, disunity.

Where they differed from us is first of all that they thought, by and large, that they *had* unity. *Dis*unity was what might come upon you. And, secondly, much as they might fear it, it did not seem to them to be one of the most pressing of human troubles. We, on the other hand, almost automatically stick "disunity" on the list of major anxieties and we are pretty sure that we have it already.

May I illustrate this from our thinking about the unity of the Church? In all our present conversations, schemes, and negotiations one of the major problems is that there are no precedents. Men have not behaved, they have not even really thought, in this way before. One can go back to the early Church, to Fathers like Cyprian once more, and one will find that they write profound and moving things about the nature of Christian unity. This may help us to understand the kind of Church and the kind of unity we are looking for. It does not help us directly to reach that goal, for the Fathers assume without exception that they can pick out the one, true, visible organization called the Church and that disunity is the result of breaking away from it. It doesn't really matter where one looks. One may take a man whom the textbooks now describe as having been a Modalist, a Montanist, or a Monophysite. The man himself believed that his denomination (if I may call it that) was the one, true Church. The others were breaking away. At the time of the Reformation the same thing is true. Luther did not believe that there could be more than one right answer or that there could be more than one Church. Everyone still took the line that there was one, true Church—that I belong to it and that you have broken away from it. I quote: "*They* establish outwardly what God neither commands nor forbids, but *they* forbid images, churches, and altars. *They* will not speak of the mass or sacrifice or elevation. *They* wear no chasuble but only a grey cloak. *They* reject all titles. *They* would kill a godless priest and refuse to be patient under injustice. And if you don't agree with them you are condemned as a double-dyed Papist, a scribe, and a murderer."[1] This is not a Roman cardinal attacking Luther, but Luther attacking the Anabaptists.

These attitudes, which see oneself as belonging to the visible Church and everyone else as breaking away from it, have persisted until very recently. Only gradually have most of us come to believe that the Church is something much wider and greater than our denominations and that the divisions are *within* the Church not *away from* it. This represents an enormous revolution in thinking. And, for those who have gone through the revolution in thought and who think of divisions *within* instead of *away from*, there has been precisely the change about which I spoke earlier. Men used to think of unity as something they possessed. On the whole disunity was thought of as a threat rather than a present reality, or as something done to you by other people rather than as a condition of human existence. Now, for us, unity is an ideal for which we (sometimes hopelessly) long and disunity is the ever present reality with which we have to live every day, no one's personal fault or responsibility, one of the destructive and frustrating characteristics of life.

The same sort of change, for different reasons in different spheres, seems to have taken place in the world as a whole. Human disunity receives its most marked outward and visible sign in war—the sacrament of disunity, so to speak. It used to be possible to mark the frontiers of war personally, geographically, or temporally. There was a time when one did not make war on women, or children, or on the clergy. There was a time when

[1] Luther, *Against the Heavenly Prophets.*

people in England would not know if there was a war in Cambodia. There was a time when you really could tell the difference between war and peace; when you could say that it was seven years since the war ended.

These things are no longer true. War has become total and impersonal. It is no longer possible to discriminate, even in favour of the clergy! The disaster of war has become total and this very totality is the one sanction we possess in our attempts to limit war. Two quite small nations equipped with nuclear weapons could not use them without dragging down their neighbours into destruction with them. Large nations have to think twice about unleashing this sort of horror upon their own, relatively comfortable, societies. So there are still rules for the game, but they are different rules. The early medieval rules compelled both sides to spare the clergy and to cease fighting on holy days. Modern rules say you can use flamethrowers on women and children but you must not use germs or nuclear weapons. What lies behind the rules is the fear of total destruction. But the fear is only strong enough to blur the edges. We do not know whether we are at peace or not. A lawyer, a university student, a politician would give different answers to the question, "Is the United States of America a nation at war?" We are never wholly at peace. We dare not go wholly to war. We are constantly made aware of the sacrament of human disunity. We live with it all the time, half-present, somewhere, affecting us whether we are directly involved or not, always in the air, unlimited except by its own potential. Again, disunity has become a condition of existence, something we have.

And the same sort of thing is true of the world generally, apart from war. For the world we live in is both bigger and smaller than ever before. It is bigger in the sense that it is a total world covering the whole globe. It is smaller in the sense that transport and communications are quicker and more effective than ever before. Whereas the medieval villager hardly moved more than a mile or two from his birthplace and never met any examples of society different from his own, we are part of a mobile and plural society, in contact with and affected by anything that happens in any other part of the world. We are forced up against people very different from ourselves and the possibilities of friction are much greater. And even if we stay put in our birthplace—I speak as a recent immigrant—other strange people come and land themselves on our doorstep. We cannot any longer escape the differences that exist within humanity and the disunity which follows from them. We are again compelled to take note of the constant existence of disunity. It is something that is always with us.

I ought to make it plain, I think, that it is not the diversity of humanity which is the trouble. Diversity we ought to look at a little more fully later. The point I am concerned to make at present is that people of very different background, culture, habits, speech and appearance are being brought together with a fair degree of frequency and permanence, and whether they like it or not. The differences can be irritants in themselves or they can be used by prejudice as a pretext. If immigrants move into an area in fairly large numbers the original inhabitants will be alarmed, as any animal is alarmed at an invasion of its territory. Foreign ways and customs will seem heathen, unhygienic, or whatever. They may actually be so. If the original inhabitants also lose their jobs, and unemployment reaches a dangerous level, it will be said that the reason is that the immigrants are prepared to work for a lower wage because they aren't used to a decent standard of living. Whether this is the real reason for unemployment or not hardly matters. Being forced into proximity with people who are very different from oneself is often not the actual cause of disunity. It provides the occasion for it.

Let us leave this point now—accepting that, in the past quarter of a century in particular, disunity has become a greater problem, and one which obtrudes more obviously, and which seems to be more an inevitable condition of human existence, than has usually been the case in previous generations.

The next point to consider is whether it is either possible or desirable to try to reverse the process and reduce the obviousness of disunity. This is not so unusual as it sounds. The policy of apartheid in my native South Africa is an attempt, in theory, to separate peoples of different race and culture so that friction is reduced because they are not always having their noses rubbed in their diversity. Mr Enoch Powell's suggestion that the repatriation of immigrants should be encouraged and assisted is another attempt to put the clock back or make the problem less obtrusive. I suppose that the Monroe doctrine and American isolationism was yet another attempt to keep the disunity of the world at arm's length. I am sure that the agreement sometimes entered into by the various denominations in the mission field, whereby each undertook not to intrude into the territory of the others, came into this category.

All these ways of thinking are really giving expression to a perfectly natural desire to reverse the tendencies we have been looking at. To shut oneself off from the rest of the world, to get rid of the obvious symptoms of difference, to achieve unity and peace by somehow reverting from this complex, plural, global society to a simpler, unitary one, must have its appeal. It is said that inside every fat man there is the thin man he would like to be. I think that inside every Englishman living in an urban, technological, plural society, there is the rustic, simple countryman that he *thinks* he would like to be. What kind of street in modern Britain gets called Elmwood Drive? Why would one, if one were trying to market an artefact, call it Meadowland Margarine? For, to be serious, we all have an image of that simple, uncomplicated, localized, peasant existence which would liberate us from problems (such as disunity) which are so obvious in the world in which we really live. That is one of the reasons why so many people are suckers for country-suggestive advertising. That is one of the reasons why so many people fall for the absence-makes-the-heart-grow-fonder political theories like *apartheid*. We want to go back to simpler days in which we were all alike.

I wonder very much whether attempts to reverse the process ever work. Satisfactory examples are not, at any rate, easy to come by. And those that one can find seldom seem to be morally defensible. Moreover, one wonders how many of us would really enjoy being flung back into the simple, uncomplicated, peasant existence of the middle ages if it became a live option instead of a hypothetical one. It seems clear that the problems are not to be solved by trying to reverse the process. The problems can only be solved by accepting the situation as it is, analysing the factors causing disunity and trying to overcome them.

In the endless debate about why God allows pain and suffering, Christian apologists have often pointed out that pain has a useful purpose.[1] Without it I might absentmindedly sit down on a red hot stove and do myself a serious mischief before I noticed the

[1] e.g. Austin Farrer, *Love Almighty and Ills Unlimited* (Collins 1962), pp. 87f.

smell of burning. This is an important thing. I think it is possible
to conceive of two kinds of universe. In one everything would be
regimented, safe, comfortable, organized—a sort of welfare
state on a vast scale. Nothing could go wrong because we were
all being properly looked after. The other kind of universe is the
one we have got. There are endless possibilities; and there are
endless possibilities of disaster. The real problem about God and
suffering is not, as it is usually put, "How can a loving father
allow his children to suffer?" The real problem, as those of us
with teenage children will know, is, "How can a loving father
not give his children sufficient freedom to suffer if they wish."

I want no part of a universe from which all the possibilities of
glory and suffering and compassion and romance have been
organized away. The whole of the younger generation is in revolt
against the dullness of the kind of world that God did not give us.
Humanity has a magnificently rich diversity. When it is brought
into contact with itself the diversity often causes friction; there
is disunity; the disunity is sometimes sacramentalized in violence
and war. What is happening is that we are receiving the danger
signals, like pain. You can try to make the world safe, but duller,
by reversing the process. I doubt whether you will succeed and
you may not like what you get in the end. Or you can go on,
preserving the richness and the diversity, the passion and the
depth, but creating a unity out of it. In our modern, urban,
technological, plural, overcrowded existence, regimentation and
over-organization are the greatest threats to our existence as
human beings. The diversity which has come at the same time
may deliver us from the appalling dullness that hangs over us.
There is undoubtedly the danger of disunity. We are being
challenged to surmount both these difficulties by setting them off
against each other, so that we may create a diversified, adventur-
ous, corporate life which is nevertheless a unity.

I am sure this is true in the field of church unity. No one wants
a united Church which is reduced to a flat level of uniformity. The
Church has an exuberant, proliferating life which is killed by any
attempt to reduce it to uniformity, but which needs, nevertheless,
to be held within a unity. I suspect that the same thing is true of
human life as a whole.

It is no part of my task to discuss the solution of this problem.
But, in the one particular field of *church* unity, I want to suggest

very briefly what I believe to be the proper approach to the problem.

In South Africa there are a good many people who believe it to be important to prove that apartheid can be justified on biblical grounds. One popular form of the argument is based on Genesis 11, the story of the tower of Babel. Genesis tells us, they say, that God punished human pride by cursing humanity with a linguistic disunity. Language is part of the cultural pattern. Genesis 11 is plainly saying, therefore, that God desires each cultural group to develop in separation and along its own lines. Hence apartheid is the will of God.

I must explain that all this is offered with an enormous solemnity and with a literal seriousness which I cannot hope to match. I can understand Babel only as saying something, as symbol and parable, about the human condition. I also believe, with St Augustine, that the Acts account of Pentecost has something to say on the subject. There is a sense in which Pentecost, with the proclamation of a message that transcends linguistic and cultural boundaries, is saying that in the Church the differences of Babel no longer matter. It is not saying that Babel is reversed or undone. The differences are still there. But there is now a common life, a common message, a common power strong enough to hold all those men and women together in a unity in which the diversities remain.[1]

This, I think, is an enormously important point to reflect upon. One can achieve a strong unit in one of two ways. One may reduce it, as it were, to its basic essential integer, so that there is nothing left to come off. That is a unit which is undifferentiated, singular, indivisible because it is a sort of prime number. The other kind of unit may be highly differentiated within itself, made up of any number of factors, diversified, comprehensive— but held together by some bond or force so strong that the components are prevented from flying off on their own. If one looks at forms of life, then the amoeba is of the first kind—man is more like the second. If one thinks in terms of what I have been arguing in this paper, those who would reverse the process want the first kind of unity. I have been asking for the second. Babel, if you like, destroyed the first kind. Pentecost created the second.

[1] cf. Augustine, *Sermons*, 269 and 271. The whole of this section of this chapter owes a great deal to Augustinian ideas.

But note that the second kind of unity depends entirely on the strength of the binding force. The more highly diversified you wish the unit to be the more powerful the binding force has to be also. Acts presents us with a picture of a Christian community bound together in a common life so powerful that it can only be described in terms of earthquake, tornado, fire. Keble's hymn entirely misses the point when it says, "The fires that rushed on Sinai down, in sudden torrents dread, Now gently light, a glorious crown, on every sainted head." The point really was that on the feast of Pentecost there was read in the synagogues the story of God's appearance to Moses on Sinai in lightning, earthquake, and thunder.[1] Acts is precisely not saying, "Here is a much tamer and gentler God". It is saying, "This curious power that had got hold of you is the same incredible power that tore Mount Sinai up in little pieces. It is the most powerful force in the world."

It is this most powerful force which we need to bind us together in the Church, preserving our diversity not destroying it. When unity schemes are being planned it is a commitment to this power, rather than a concentration upon uniformity which ought to be our chief concern. I do not for a moment doubt that a concern for confessional statements, liturgical standards, a proper ordering of the ministry, and other matters of this kind will be a necessary part of any scheme. Structures and organizations are tremendously important just because, if they go wrong, they can be so destructive. But no attempt at unity must lose sight of the real and much more difficult matter of the binding force which is capable of holding the Church together in spite of an exuberant and proliferating diversity.

It is difficult to give an example in this brief chapter which will not seem trite and facile, but I believe that there is one in the unions recently inaugurated in North India and Pakistan. This union includes both those who conscientiously hold that baptism ought only to be administered to those who are able to make a conscious proclamation of their personal faith and those who, equally conscientiously, hold that it is proper to baptize infants.[2]

[1] R. G. Finch, *The Synagogue Lectionary and the New Testament* (S.P.C.K. 1939), pp. 83f.
[2] *Plan of Church Union in North India and Pakistan*, proposed constitution, section VI. 4.

At first sight one might think that this was an intractable problem that could not honestly be solved and it is plain that the Christians involved have, indeed, been through an agonizing process in wrestling with it. In the end they were able to agree to allow a theological and practical diversity because "profession of faith is required of those baptized in infancy before admission to membership in full standing in the Church, thereby acknowledging the nature of the Church as the fellowship of believers".[1] In other words neither group has given up its conscientiously held belief. There is no covering up of the difficulties or of the diversity. But they have seen through the differences to the vital thing, which is the realization that a willing devotion of one's whole self to the Christian life is at the heart of baptism. That common understanding, one hopes and prays, will be a sufficiently strong bond to allow the diversity to exist within the one Church.

To have seen that commitment or devotion to a particular kind of life is more important even than conscientiously held theological differences may seem a simple thing. In practice it cannot have been easy to have reached such an agreement. But there is an impatience abroad which says that the Church, as an institution, has very little appeal. Yet a living movement, committed to Christ and to Christian life, is still capable of attracting the deepest loyalty. That impatience has got its priorities right. It is telling us that, in the Church as in society, we *can* achieve a unity which is rich in diversity provided that there is a bond powerful enough to enable us to enjoy human differences instead of being terrified by them. For the Church that bond is the Holy Spirit.

FOR FURTHER READING

I suggest three or four books, which are neither sources for what I have said, nor "further reading" in the sense that they continue and develop the ideas set out here. They are simply good books which have something to say on the subject.

C. D. DARLINGTON, *The Evolution of Man and Society.* 1969.

PIERRE TEILHARD DE CHARDIN, *Man's Place in Nature* (tr. R. Hague). 1966.

DAVID E. JENKINS, *The Glory of Man.* 1967.

HANS KÜNG, *The Church* (tr. R. and R. Ockenden). 1967. (Particularly section D.)

[1] Appendix to the proposed constitution contained in the *Plan of Church Union in North India and Pakistan, 1965.*

5

The Theology of Creation

J. S. Habgood

Let us begin by concentrating first on the question, What is the doctrine of creation about? We will then look more briefly at a few of the practical implications of the doctrine, with particular reference to the growth of technology.

Doctrines are to be understood, not as isolated items of information, but as answers to questions. If interpreted as answers to the wrong questions, the results can be disastrous. For example, if the question is "How did the world come to be as it is?", any answer in terms of "creation" immediately puts the doctrine in the realm of pseudo-scientific assertion—where for many people it remains. Much of the unprofitable controversy centred round the subject has derived purely and simply from this basic mistake.

But if this is not the right question about creation, what is? I suggest that there are at least three to which doctrine gives an answer, and these questions remain real and important ones, whether or not the Christian answer to them is accepted.

1. The question of meaning
2. The question of ultimate security
3. The question of newness.

1. THE QUESTION OF MEANING

This vast topic seems to be a main theme of the classic creation story in Genesis 1. When men asked about their place in the world and how they were to interpret the meaning of their existence,

49

the answer was given quite clearly in Genesis. The world is God's; it is wholly dependent on him; its meaning is not to be found in itself, but in a reality outside it. It is an orderly world, where man occupies a definite position in relation to other creatures. It is intelligible, with the implication that man can know his place and explore its ramifications. Man can thus become scientific man. The world is also usable; man is given dominion over it and can share something of God's creativity; he can become technological man.

Within this clear answer to the question of meaning there was an implicit recognition of the balance to be maintained between man's involvement within nature and his use of it as a means for his own ends. The men who accepted this answer knew where they belonged and knew the limits of their power.

Today, even among those who will accept the traditional answers, there has been a shift of emphasis for which two main factors seem to have been responsible. The first has been the development of a new kind of relationship with nature, following the rise of the natural sciences. This has been called "the onlooker attitude". To a scientific onlooker nature is an objective reality outside himself, a set of external phenomena to be studied as far as possible without personal involvement. Such a detached view of things is an essential element in the scientific attitude and I would not for one moment wish to deny its importance. But it has by-products; it has encouraged a feeling for the world as a collection of objects with no inherent value in themselves, available for men to manipulate. The onlooker thinks *about* phenomena; he has lost that whole dimension in which nature is a reality to be felt and responded to, rather than merely studied. The Romantic movement was one attempt to redress the balance. In our own day, concern with such concepts as "alienation" and "participation" seems to fulfil the same sort of function.

The second factor which has upset the traditional balance has been the startling increase in man's actual power. Three hundred years ago it could not be said for certain that man was the biologically dominant species on earth. Today he can put in jeopardy every other species, as well as himself. We are constantly being reminded that the scale of man's exploitation of his environment has now reached disastrous proportions. Whereas once upon a time to tell man that he had "dominion over the earth" could bring encouragement in what was in fact a hard struggle, now it is vital that "dominion" should be interpreted as a limiting concept in a situation of responsibility.

Whether these two are the only factors operative or not is immaterial. Our problem nowadays is to give an answer to the question of meaning which allows full weight to actual human achievements, without cutting off man's roots in nature and seeming to set him up as some lonely alienated power over it.

Teilhard de Chardin's evolutionary theology is an obvious example of an attempt to do just this. Teilhard's aim, as he said, was "to make room for thought in the world", to produce a scientific synthesis which did not leave man cut off from the object of his study in isolated irresponsibility, but used him as a clue to the understanding of the process in which he was involved. His final answer, though purportedly derived from science, was surprisingly similar to the traditional one. In Teilhard's thought, the world is dependent on God as the goal towards which it is moving. It is an orderly world because, despite immense profusion, evolution has a direction. One stage of development builds upon another until the process reaches its present climax in man. It is an intelligible world; in fact in man the evolutionary process becomes conscious of itself. And the world is therefore usable. Man has the immense responsibility of taking the helm of evolution, but he does so as a product of evolution, as part of the process. The greater the emphasis on the unity of the process, the greater the need to treat all parts of it with respect.

This is not the place to elaborate these views. I simply mention them to illustrate the point that the question of meaning, as posed in terms of man's relationship to nature, still arouses enormous contemporary interest. A similar reappraisal of the question can be made by starting from the theological end, and this is perhaps where a phrase from the Lambeth Conference Report—"Christ, the agent of all creation"—may provide a useful clue. [1]

On the face of it such a phrase sounds nonsensical. Without having the space to argue a whole theological position, I would wish to interpret it by claiming that for Christians the paradigm

[1] "A theology of creation needs to be worked out which sees Christ, the agent of all Creation, as inaugurating a cosmic redemption." (*The Lambeth Conference Report 1968* (S.P.C.K.), p. 75.)

of God's activity is Christ; and this is no less true for the doctrine of creation than for any other doctrine. If the clue to creation is Christ, then the God we call Creator is not one who stands apart from his creation to make it what it is by acts of arbitrary power; he is himself involved and hidden. His involvement is of such a kind as to allow maximum freedom to his creatures, even the freedom to reject him and push him out of his own world. His power is the power of love which expresses itself most characteristically in bringing good out of evil, and life out of death.

For Christians who think in these terms the answer to the question of meaning is quite simply—Christ: Christ as the representative of God's presence within the world, and as the pointer to the world's consummation beyond itself. The Creator God is the one who in humility lets the world be itself, but is a loving, life-giving, reconciling presence within it. Those who understand the world christocentrically must therefore themselves respect the freedom and integrity of the whole creation and reflect in their actions the loving, life-giving, reconciling work of God.

These are high abstractions, presented summarily and dogmatically. My aim is to provide a survey, not detailed arguments. But already, I hope, an attitude towards nature is emerging, whose practical implications will be considered later.

2. THE QUESTION OF ULTIMATE SECURITY

This is another dominant concern of the Genesis creation narratives. Underlying the stories was the primitive fear of chaos, the sense that the world was a precarious balance between good and evil, that flood and disaster could sweep all man's achievements away. There are hints of still deeper fears about the abyss of nothingness into which everything might fall, fears which are not wholly absent in our own day.

Against these fears the faith of the Bible is firm. God is the one whose spirit broods over the darkness of chaos and says, "Let there be light." He is the one who "holds up the pillars of the earth", who promises that "while earth remains, seed-time and harvest shall not cease . . .". Whatever the threats, however devastating the precariousness of life, there is an ultimate security, ultimate reliability, in God. Man can feel at home; he can rejoice in his successes and bear his losses because there is an ultimate stability about the order of things.

A traditional means of expressing such ideas was through the doctrine of God's changelessness, and this in turn was linked with philosophical interpretations of the doctrine of creation based on the notion of change. Change, so the argument went, can only ultimately be understood in terms of what is unchanging. The idea of absolute change is nonsensical. If, for instance, there were no unchanging constants in nature, our hope of understanding it would be nil. What then, it was asked, is the ultimate unchangeable? What is the still point about which the turning world revolves?

Philosophically this is not an argument to be despised. But religiously, I suspect, its effect has been disastrous. When the question of ultimate security is answered in terms of changelessness, and changelessness is given a primarily philosophical meaning, there develops a concept of God as not in any real sense affected by the world, and so not in any Christian sense involved in it. If the ultimate reality is changeless, then history does not matter, and it becomes impossible to think of God as giving meaning to the world by being personally concerned about what happens.

Such thoughts have led to a strong reaction against traditional theology at this point. One of the strongest alternative candidates is Process Theology, which already has a large following in the United States. It is a way of thinking about God as involved in creation which has proved very attractive to Christians who wish to emphasize a dynamic evolutionary perspective. Many of those who write nowadays on the relationship between science and religion acknowledge their debt to such a theology. But my own belief is that in the end it fails to give an adequate account of God's transcendence.

A christocentric doctrine of creation should emphasize that God is changeless love; that our security is based upon the grace of God, and nothing else; and that therefore the real conflicts and tragedies of life can be accepted and given meaning in terms of our relationship with God, not because he is unaffected by them, but because his grace is sufficient for us.

There can be no guarantee that any particular human enterprise will be successful, or that any part of the universe is safe from

disaster. The pattern of evolution reveals enormous changes and
staggering waste. Security, in the naive sense, is minimal. But
just as seeing the world in terms of creation is to be open constantly to the element of surprisingness in it, so at every point
in the process there are similar possibilities of surprise. Tragedy
is not bypassed, but overcome. Death is not nullified, but used
as the basis for more life. Ultimate security depends, not on
some external stability, but on the inexhaustibility of God's grace.

This, I believe, is the essence of Karl Barth's assertion "Creation
in grace". It seems to follow inevitably from the phrase we have
already considered, "Christ, the agent of all creation". Interpreted
as a claim to knowledge about some mysterious intermediary
in the creative process, the phrase can only be misleading. Its
true meaning is quite simply that the basis of our assurance about
the world is the same as the basis of our assurance about God.
We have received the grace of God in the person of Jesus Christ.

The practical implications of such an answer to the question of
ultimate security can be summed up in words like "receptiveness"
and "gratitude". Once again I shall leave the further discussion of
these to a later section.

3. THE QUESTION OF NEWNESS

Here we come to the most obvious of the questions to which the
doctrine of creation is an answer, but also to the most dangerous
one. Newness needs an explanation, whether new ideas, new
events, new inventions, or new creation in some absolute sense.
And the classic biblical explanation of newness is God. "Behold,
I do a new thing. . . . If any man is in Christ, he is a new creation.
. . . I make all things new. . . ." The list of references is endless.
Wherever there is discontinuity we are apt to invoke the creative
power of God, or the creative power of the artist, or simply
creative as a mysterious irreducible cause.

The dangers inherent in such an approach have been fully
revealed in the history of the relation between science and
religion. Quasi-scientific explanations of this kind in terms of
ultimate mystery have an alarming habit of becoming more and
more tenuous and remote as knowledge advances.

The alternative explanation of newness is to deny that there is
anything essentially new to explain. Everything emerges out of

what preceded it by a progressive recombination of elements which were already there. The newness of species, say, in evolutionary history can be accounted for if their history is divided into a series of sufficiently small steps, each of which follows the other as a result of some minimal change ascribable to chance.

One of the most impressive theories of newness uses the general idea of evolution as a model. Take a certain number of elements, they may be genes or ideas or anything else, mix them up randomly, and then use some screening device to select out of the enormous number of possible combinations those which are favourable, or useful, or come up to whatever other criterion has been chosen. This is the principle of biological evolution, the random mutation of genes coupled with the natural selection of those best fitted to survive. It is the basis of computer learning and deciding mechanisms; introduce a randomizer at an appropriate point in the operation and then let the computer do the work of selecting which new combinations are worth preserving. Newness emerges out of this process, not by the introduction of some mysterious element of creativity, but simply because the process is a way of exploring every possibility, and some possibilities must in the nature of the case have been previously untried, and hence be new.

Such an account, atheistic though it may sound, can be reconciled reasonably well with theology. God lets creation be itself, as he must if his creatures are themselves to have genuine freedom as creators and innovators and decision-makers. Freedom can only exist where, built into some stable, reliable structure, there is a mechanism for throwing up endless alternative possibilities, something equivalent to the randomizer in a computer. Within the orderly framework of the universe, the element of chance and accident may perform precisely this function. These are to be seen, then, no longer as unfortunate blemishes in an otherwise purposeful system, but as the very means which God has designed to ensure continual newness, and hence the continual possibility of freedom.

The main trouble about this kind of reductionist explanation of newness is not its apparent anti-theological slant. It is that, although it takes us a long way, it does not seem to take us quite far enough. In particular it gives us no help in understanding any sense in which the universe itself can have been said to be new.

Whatever else the doctrine of creation may be said to be about, it is certainly not about the reshuffling of what already existed. Nor does human creativity, as we actually experience it, seem to fit comfortably into this rather restricted pattern. Even on the comparatively simple level of evolutionary theory, it is possible that there is more to be said; it seems likely that behaviour, an organism's own ability to respond in fresh ways to its environment, plays a greater part in natural selection than the simple account would indicate.

On the positive side, a reductionist explanation emphasizes that, even if in the last resort creating new things is more than reshuffling old things, there is nevertheless an essential connection between old and new. Newness does not just appear. The new is in some sense a transformation of the old, an explanation of it. But in the process of transformation there may also have been a leap, the discovery of a new perspective or movement to a new level, from which the old is seen or experienced differently, freshly.

It may sound fantastic to claim that any light could be shed on such questions by considering the relation between the Old and New Testaments. But for a Christian who believes seriously that Christ is indeed the clue to creation the relation between the two Testaments must be a good deal more than a matter of historical interest. It raises the most fundamental questions about the nature of the Gospel. In what sense was Christ new? In what sense did he fulfil the Old Testament? or destroy it? or transform it? The newness of Christ himself, as "the agent of all creation", must somehow be the paradigm in terms of which all newness is to be understood. To the objection that all this is a far cry from creation in the sense of "the origin of all things", the answer must be that all traditional talk about origins eventually draws on analogies from human creativity, so that it is surely not inappropriate to look at one of the great creative moments in history. Furthermore, if we think in terms of the creative process rather than of some unimaginable original act at the beginning of time, the relationship between old and new is the key question.

It is the key also, I believe, to our attitude towards those practical problems which must soon concern us. If we hold that creation is essentially something mysterious and disruptive; if our main understanding of Christ is that he breaks in and shatters

all that went before him, then presumably we shall be pente-
costalists or revolutionaries. We shall not be afraid of the loss of
the old, because for us it is incomparably less than the glory of the
new. If, on the other hand, we see creation as a delicate process of
building up complex structures, physical, social, mental, within
which the new can emerge; if our main understanding of Christ
is that he gave a new meaning to the tradition to which he
belonged by transforming and expanding it, then presumably we
shall be conservative reformers. I know this is a grossly over-
simplified contrast. But it illustrates the kind of connection worth
looking for between our theological and philosophical thinking
on a subject like creation, and those attitudes of mind and value
judgements which determine how we actually react to the startling
novelties of our world.

So far I have tried to sketch in three answers to the three fundamental questions of creation. To the question of ultimate meaning,
the Christian answer is Christ. To the question of ultimate security
the Christian answer is the Grace of God as manifested in Christ.
To the question of newness, the Christian answer is Christ is the
paradigm of newness. And these three answers together make up
what I understand to be "a theology of creation which sees Christ,
the agent of all creation, as inaugurating a cosmic redemption".
I now intend to apply these answers to a few of the ethical
problems which prompted the bishops' request to theology. I have
already said some obvious things about love, receptiveness,
gratitude, reconciliation, responsibility, and power. I have
referred to the need to reinterpret biblical language about man's
dominion over the earth in the light of the dangerous excess of
power which he now has. In what follows I shall take all this for
granted, and concentrate on a number of themes which have not
been so central in recent discussions.

1. OUR ATTITUDE TOWARDS "THINGS"

To ask how a man thinks about the world of "things" is another
way of asking what I have called "the question of meaning". It
is a way which draws attention to a disturbing feature of modern
life. There are those who make such a radical distinction between
persons and things that their world ceases to be one. The theology
of *I-Thou* and *I-it* is one symptom of this split. While I have no

Ccc

wish to deny its value, I nevertheless believe that it has left us curiously incapable of making ethical decisions about the world of "things" at a time when "things" are becoming more and more important to us. By "things" in this context I mean primarily artefacts. Natural objects as well as artefacts have an element of "thinghood" about them, and are experienced in *I-it* relationships, but not all these relationships are of the same quality. We seem to recognize different degrees of autonomy, and modify our behaviour accordingly. Mountains, trees, rivers, wild animals, have all in their time been exploited, and still are. But increasing numbers of people are developing a conscience about them. As we have already seen, there is also a growing awareness that, as creatures rooted in this natural world, men must have respect and sensitivity towards it.

Artefacts, on the other hand, are the things which our own hands have made, and this is the classic Old Testament description of an idol. Christians have been quick to point out the dangers of materialism and acquisitiveness and overdependence in a world increasingly dominated by artefacts, to such an extent that guilt about our affluent society is confused with guilt about a technological society as such. Hand in hand with a growing valuation of the world of nature has gone a growing disrespect of the world of technology, at the very time when we do in fact depend on technology to an unprecedented degree. That way lies schizophrenia.

Our ambivalent attitude to motor cars is an obvious example. It is easy to make a case against cars. They create a host of moral problems: general environmental ones—roads, pollution, accidents, traffic density, city life, the use of limited natural resources, and so on. There are less direct human problems associated with them; their relation to affluence, their use as status symbols or substitutes for power. They give rise to new social problems, indeed to new types of society. And they are even the subject of religious complaints, cars as idols to be loved and polished on Sunday mornings. Yet there can be few car-owners, however aware they might be of the trouble they were causing, who would willingly forgo having one. Life as it is actually lived in the twentieth century to a considerable extent revolves around this particular artefact. And therefore the question of our relation to it, as part of the general attitude towards "things", is an urgent one.

Are "things" mere tools, neutral, disposable, external to us and unrelated, and therefore in this sense to be distinguished from "nature"? Or have they too some sort of meaning and identity as part of creation? Is it possible to say that the works of our hands, even the mass-produced works of factory hands, are part of that total creative process which is summed up in Christ?

If the answer is that our artefacts do indeed have a meaning as part of God's work of creation, then perhaps the people who go to traction engine rallies and renovate old cars and have a feel for machinery, as others may have a feel for art, are not so odd as they are sometimes made out to be. Perhaps they have gone some way towards bringing things into our human world and humanizing them. I am not advocating salvation through veteran cars and Victorian lamp-posts. The dangers of materialism and idolatry are real. But so are the dangers of alienation, the dangers of living in a world more and more of which is intrinsically worthless and disposable. The wasteful society ought to be condemned, not only for using up limited natural resources, but also for filling so much of our lives with meaningless rubbish.

2. OUR ATTITUDE TOWARDS "NOVELTY"

This is another aspect of the same theme, though under this heading it seems best to put the emphasis, not so much on the fact that it is *we* who make our environment, as on the constant search for new forms of it. The relentless pressure towards technological novelty, the thirst for new experience (which, incidentally, seems to be one of the driving forces in our youth culture), the scientific concern with ever-expanding possibilities, all these feed our desire for novelty. "New" has become the great sales slogan.

Again the question which needs to be asked is the question of meaning: "New—for what?" Sometimes the answer is obvious, as when there are basic human needs still to be met. New methods of food production or birth control need very little justification. But the time has certainly come in some areas of our affluent societies when the question "New—for what?" is a highly relevant one. A large part of our creative and industrial energy is now spent in producing things which are new simply for the sake of newness.

This may not be wrong. There are those who would wish to justify it on economic grounds. It could also be argued, as I did when discussing evolution, that there needs to be exploration of every possibility so that what is worth preserving can be selected. Out of a thousand useless novelties may come something really worth while, which then justified the whole enterprise. But how do we judge worthwhileness? In society as it is, "worth while" tends to mean "commercially worth while" and it is financial considerations which thus give direction to the whole process.

I am only scratching the surface of a highly complex issue. The main point, however, is that if Christ is the paradigm of newness then this question "New—for what?" receives a very different kind of answer. Newness as part of God's creative plan has an end, a goal, a direction. God does new things. A Christian ought to expect and work for a progressive enrichment of human life. He ought to be prepared to see in technological advance, and in the exercise of human power, signs of God's activity. Those who believe in Christ ought also to believe in the infinite possibilities of being human, because humanity in Christ is open to the perspective of God. But if newness is thus claimed as part of God's plan, it also has to be admitted that like everything human it is ambiguous when set in the context of eternity. New possibilities are temptations as well as opportunities. Trying everything, exploring everything, can be a recipe for destruction as well as creation. Technological advance, if treated as an end in itself, can just as easily increase human misery and division, as lead to happiness and unity. "New—for what?" is a question which has to be asked again and again, in the most awkward and persistent way possible, by those who believe that the kind of newness which ultimately matters was revealed once for all in the new, yet old, activity of God in Christ; in a dying rising life, where newness met its true cost. There is a magnificent sentence in the second-century Epistle to Diognetus which in my opinion not only sums up the mystery of Christ, but points the way to a profound and balanced attitude to this concept of the new. "This is he [speaking of Christ] who was from the beginning, who appeared new and was found to be old, and is ever born young in the hearts of the saints."

3. OUR ACCEPTANCE OF "LIMITS"

This theme, like the last one, follows on from what I have just been saying. It echoes a phrase used by the Lambeth bishops—"disciplined restraint". If newness is not an end in itself, how do we set the limits? What sort of restraints ought there to be, say, on the processes of invention and production?

I remember once at a gathering of very responsibly-minded scientists suggesting that there must be times in scientific research when somebody says stop. The result was explosive. I had committed the unpardonable heresy of trying to clip Prometheus's wings. Like the comedians who went to the top of the Post Office Tower "because it was there", the committed scientist is apt to see the mere existence of a possibility as sufficient reason for trying to realize it.

This is where the perspective of grace can help us to view the matter differently. Though invention and discovery seem to open the door to unlimited achievements, they do so in a world which is ours by grace, not by right of possession. And the goals we aim at are goals set by limited, finite beings who in their turn live by grace. And if this is more than a form of words, it ought to mean that built into our processes of technological advance there should be a deep self-questioning, a denial of God-likeness, a readiness to admit our ignorance and shortsightedness, and not to prejudice the future by acting too far in advance of our understanding.

None of this is easy to apply directly to our ordinary scientific or commercial procedures. Nor is it possible to define precisely what the limits are, or where and how we should exercise restraint. It is more a matter of atmosphere and basic assumption. It seems probable that at different times the limits should rightly be set in different places. What may be irresponsible arrogance in one period of history may be a matter of ordinary safe routine in another. Some of the most valuable discussions of heart transplants, for example, concentrated on this kind of issue.

But the point is that for us here and now as finite human beings to know that there *are* limits, to live under restraint, is an essential part of being human. We are, in a word, creatures. And perhaps in the end that is the most important conclusion to be drawn from any theology of creation.

FOR FURTHER READING

L. C. BIRCH, *Nature and God.* 1965.

HUGH MONTEFIORE, *The Question Mark.* 1969.

IAN G. BARBOUR (ed.), *Science and Religion.* 1968.

6

Inter-Faith Dialogue

John B. Taylor

THE NEED FOR DIALOGUE

A deepening conviction of many Christians today is that we should look both within and beyond the frontiers of the Church for signs of God's saving and healing initiatives. Statements of the World Council of Churches, the Vatican Council, the Lambeth Conference and, perhaps still more significant, the voices of the younger Churches in Asia and Africa are urging us Christians into a new dialogue with the world.

A significant and widely acclaimed part of this dialogue is with the secular world; the Church is rightly involved in social, political, and ideological issues. Yet inter-religious dialogue is also seen as increasingly clamant, not least in the third world.

Dialogue may involve a rediscovered theology of incarnation and participation which urges us as adopted sons to try, perhaps belatedly, to do what our Lord did in identifying with the world's joys and sufferings. It may be a theology of mission which leads us to go first to where our neighbour stands rather than summoning him to our position and leaving him alone if he cannot come. It may be a theology of hope which expects the Spirit's activity in the most unlikely places and believes that all things work together for good.

It has been a salutary discovery of recent years that Christians must take seriously the religious vitality and integrity of so-called non-Christian peoples. We had at many points developed an insidious exclusivism which assumed that progress all over the world must lie in the emulation of the cultural and religious values of Western Christendom.

We see now that there are family loyalties in animist Africa, legal rights in the Muslim world, artistic achievements and spiritual insights in Hindu and Buddhist traditions, industrial originality in modern Japan, which owe little or nothing to Westernization or deliberate Christianization. Furthermore, the very concept of Western Christendom may be anomalous and arrogant when, as so often, it takes no account of the heritage of rich spirituality in the Eastern Churches, nor yet of the exciting influx of social, political and humanitarian practicality in the younger Churches of Africa and Asia.

In discerning the activity of the Holy Spirit throughout world history we do not begrudge a sense of gratitude for much that has been achieved for mankind by Western Christians. Yet we do not forget that Western Christian countries have themselves been enriched by some of the extraneous opportunities of European and North American geography, by local and imperial material wealth, and by a political and intellectual heritage which extends from pre-Christian Greece to post-Christian secularism. The many ways in which Christian theology and Christian society integrated and exploited these world-views point to the danger of categorizing any movement as "non-Christian" because it lay earlier or later than centuries of ecclesiastical influence, because it originated in other areas, or because it stemmed from another religious tradition. One might even reject the entire concept of the "non-Christian" in so far as it is a human judgement which limits God to the confines of a Church which is so often tardy in its missionary expansion.

The myopic equation of modernization with Westernization is convincingly eroded when we are confronted with the rediscovery of self-confidence in other religious traditions. We find that the implications of secularizing processes are well understood by modernist Muslims who have always rejected a division between the sacred and the secular; they see secularization as a practical and spiritual in-worldly commitment to political and social reform, and in no way do they assume that it must entail an atheistic ideology of secularism. The religious outlook upon human relationships preached by Gandhi reminds us that religious values and emotions are ineradicable in a predominantly peasant world; he shows us that they can be constructive too. Religious revival and Islamic cultural roots in secular Turkey endorse the Turkish sociologists' analysis that it was not the spiritual and cultural aspects of Islam which impeded modern Turkey, but legalistic and hierarchical traditions. In different contemporary contexts, in the religious cults of Nkrumah and Mao Tse-tung, we have seen the blasphemous results when men or ideologies aspire to supplant God.

Religious divisions and the suspicions and tensions engendered between religious groups may indeed be inhibiting to modern progress. But it is this divisiveness and not the religions themselves whereby the problems are created. Christian presence, usually as a tiny minority in the context of other world religions, even as in the context of materialism and apathy, calls everywhere for a patience, a humility, and a commitment to reconciliation and to disinterested service from Christians towards their neighbours. The Church must always exist as leaven in the lump. One recalls too that Jesus taught the supreme lesson of loving one's neighbour by citing the example of a man in another religious tradition, the Samaritan. One of the chastening experiences of exposing oneself to the claims of other religions is that one is led to re-examine and perhaps to re-awaken one's own.

Only as we show our readiness to meet with and to learn from the men of other faiths shall we use a common sense of our human creatureliness under God for a common resolve to serve him through our service of our fellow men. If we explore the openings for inter-religious dialogue we shall find that this conviction is held by men of various faiths. If we can see this as part of the guidance of the Holy Spirit, we may be impelled to a new understanding of Christian responsibility, to a new understanding of Christian mission.

My own specialization is in Islamic Studies. Accordingly I propose to look especially at Christians' dialogue with Muslims. This may serve to illustrate the predicament and the opportunity of the Church over against other resurgent missionary religions. Muslims have shown themselves consistently and effectively immune to any attempts at proselytization. Their claim to a universal and final revelation constitutes a direct challenge, but not necessarily a negative threat, to Christians. Christian-Muslim dialogue is made particularly relevant by virtue of the almost universal juxtaposition of Muslims with Christians in the Middle East, in South East Asia, in India and Pakistan, throughout Africa, among immigrants in Europe and Britain, not to mention the heterodox Black Muslims in the U.S.A.; everywhere we are neighbours, but we are rarely neighbourly. Our relationship with Islam is made yet more poignant by the Muslims' partial recognition of Christ and by their claiming a place in the same prophetic and monotheistic tradition.

The lessons which we learn from studying Islam cannot at all points apply to our attitude to all other faiths. There are areas of common ground in our understanding of God and of our fellow men which do not apply to animist or non-theistic traditions. But in the intentions and the principles of dialogue which we apply to the Muslim situation, we may find tools to explore other possibilities for the Christian conscience to serve in fields where Christ has been hitherto unknown, unrecognized, unpreached, or rejected.

MEETING FOR DIALOGUE

Dialogue cannot take place without mutual cooperation. If we wish to talk together, we must talk with each other, not against or about each other. Controversy can push Christians and Muslims apart; one may win the argument, but lose the chance for any further inquiry or understanding. Controversy involves judgement by each other rather than mutual submission to the judgement of God.

If one's attitude may be too aggressive and too self-centred, it may also be too detached and impersonal. Comparative study of religion can be a useful academic discipline for establishing common ground and for explaining tensions. It may be dangerous if it advocates a syncretism or relativism which would evade the poignancy of our differences by compromises which are untrue to both Muslim and Christian claims of universality. We do not advocate comparison as an end in itself, but as a preparation for better understanding and co-operation.

If one experiences the universal relevance of one's own religious tradition and respects a similar missionary conviction in one's Muslim or Christian neighbour, then this may produce a more realistic dialogue than deist sentimentality or humanist solidarity.

One reason why dialogue between Muslims and Christians is entering on a new, more healthy stage, is that both traditions are newly self-confident, though not self-sufficient; neither need be on the defensive—for defensiveness breeds sterile apologetic. Dialogue involves talking together, working together, and serving God together. It is a practical form of obedience to love and serve one's neighbour, whether he belongs to one's own religious tradition, to another, or to none. This last category, those unable to find God's outreach to them, has an urgent claim upon us as religious men, whether we be Muslim or Christian.

The first thing necessary for co-operation in dialogue is that the two parties should meet together. It may seem a very obvious platitude to point out this first stage of Muslim-Christian encounter. And yet dialogue will be impossible without the firm intention to find ways to meet each other. Our communities at present so often exist with little inter-action; there is apathy where there should be mutual trust.

Christians and Muslims have for too long lived in separate compartments of society. Religious traditions have been socially divisive throughout history; there are still too many signs of this, in the tensions of the Indo-Pakistani sub-continent, in the Middle East, and in Africa. There has been brutal communal violence between Christians and Muslims in the Southern Sudan (with blame on both sides), and there has been the tragedy in Nigeria of inter-tribal butchery, profanely enlisting religious emotions. Such examples remind us that we dare not wait until religious prejudices are inflamed before submitting ourselves to the reconciling influences which faith in God can bring.

Social insulation or antagonism has a counterpart in academic isolation or arrogance in Christians' and Muslims' study of each other. Western "orientalists" at first risked storm or censure among narrow-minded colonialist fellow-westerners for their concern, and even love, for the east. Later some of them forfeited the confidence of many Muslims because they were so often content to criticize the external practices of Islamic tradition, and were so seldom ready to appreciate or encourage the ideals and aspirations of Muslims. Some succumbed to the seductive temptation to compare only the best in one's own tradition with only the worst in the other man's tradition—a complete denial of the spirit of dialogue. Not all the "orientalists" are guilty of this, but we still incur the suspicion of Muslims that our motives are aimed at undermining Islam. Personal meeting and friendship can do much to win confidence in each other's true intentions.

Theological isolation has been still worse. There are strong arguments to say that Islam arose and spread in a situation of political and spiritual vacuum in the seventh century A.D. Christians were too preoccupied with their dogmatic differences to be concerned for their animist neighbours in Arabia. When Islam did spread into the Middle East, North Africa, Spain, Iran, and India it slowly displaced Christian communities that had already grown faint-hearted or disgusted by dogmatism. There are uncomfortable parallels in the world today where the Church may have become a self-engrossed ghetto or a self-interested sect. We still express our creeds in a private language dependent for its intelligibility on a Judaic or Greek background. We still often confuse others by presenting Christianity in the trappings of Western culture. We are only slowly learning that theological language, symbols, and rituals can be accommodated to a wide variety of cultures, without compromising their essential truth.

Muslims and Christians and men in other religious traditions have been estranged from each other both socially, academically, and theologically. Many of us desire to meet each other, and to enter upon a dialogue through which we may learn from each other. We desire not only to meet and to learn, but also to serve our fellow men and to serve God.

DIALOGUE FOR LEARNING

It is not an easy process to learn sensitively about another religious tradition, or from a man whose understanding of God is different from our own. It is disturbing to find our own religious concepts challenged or misunderstood. It may be taxing and difficult to give a fair hearing to theological language which is unfamiliar, and to recognize the spiritual values in symbols and rituals which are not a part of our own tradition. There may also be barriers of prejudice which we must overcome in ourselves before we can learn.

There is no set curriculum for this inter-religious learning process. It is certainly not exclusively an enterprise for specialists in the comparative study of religion or for Islamicists. Since Islamic principles should affect every part of life, Christian men and women in many callings should seek to understand the faith and tradition of their Muslim neighbours, whose needs they hope to share and serve. Christian nurses and social workers need to understand patterns of Muslim family life. Legal and commercial transactions may be guided by Muslim principles; no one can avoid being affected by Islamic political and social ideologies.

Likewise, Muslims have not remained untouched by Christian influences. Influences do not presuppose contamination or dilution; there may be ideals or techniques which Muslims adopt of their own free will, which they Islamize and make their own. This is true for theological apologetic in medieval times and for social ethic today; it is a sign of strength in Islam that it can absorb and refashion such influences. This cross-fertilization must be understood in its historical context and in its spiritual integrity if Muslims are to avoid the impoverishment of xenophobia.

If they are to understand the richness of their own heritage, in theory and in practice, then intelligent Muslims should seek to understand something of Christian faith and tradition. There have been many Christian visions and achievements, as well as failures, in the evolution of history to the present day; for better or worse, intentionally and involuntarily, Muslims have been involved in both the contributions and abuses brought by the so-called Christian West. Both of us need to understand our past and present involvement with each other.

Ideally we should be instructed in each other's religious traditions as a basic part of our education. Whether our Muslim neighbours are a vast majority, as for a Christian in Pakistan, or whether they are still a small minority, as for us in England with our new Muslim immigrant neighbours, in either case it is desirable that Christian and Muslim children should learn about each other's cultures and be prepared to appreciate each other's spiritual insights. We may have to accept that this is impracticable until good teachers have been trained for this delicate task. But unless we start to train such teachers for schools, seminaries, and universities, we can never hope to improve the present lack of mutual respect, the ignorance that breeds arrogance.

The University of Birmingham, among others, is hoping to answer the increasing curiosity among students for study of another religious tradition. This curiosity is not motivated by exotic fancies but by a wish to take more seriously our commitment to world-wide peace and co-operation. All honours students in theology now take a course in Islamics or some other world faith. Students may take post-graduate courses to deepen their study of the faith of other men. Christian students engaged in vocational training in the Selly Oak colleges show themselves particularly open to exploring the values of, for example, Islam in the modern world. When these young people go to serve in Muslim countries, often as missionaries or among Muslim communities in Britain, they will not go to denounce or to compromise the position of Islam; they will go to live alongside Muslims and to engage in a mutually enriching service which takes its departure from a readiness to learn on both sides.

Today no one can afford to write or speak without checking or being checked by the views of the other faith. This can produce a deep sympathy for Islam among Christians, and Muslims are expressing confidence in the integrity of Christian scholars. Both sides learn to accept criticism which is offered not in a self-righteous spirit, but in the spirit of loving dialogue which must set high standards for each other precisely because of its deep concern for each other.

There can be great enrichment in such inter-religious meeting and learning. It tackles the need for a theology to account for our religious diversity. Unless we are content simply to consign each other to hell, we must be led to search for God's wisdom in our religious diversity and to confess man's folly in our divisiveness. Dialogue encourages us to penetrate into each other's spiritual experiences, to achieve sympathy with that which is sought after by our neighbour, and to realize the priorities within our own tradition. When we learn the religious terminology of the other man's faith; when we try to communicate to him our own experience of God, we are rethinking, re-expressing and, perhaps, rediscovering truth about God.

If we start by being ready to learn about our neighbour's faith and tradition, rather than by rushing in to teach our own, we may already be making an effective witness and may also be preparing for communication and even proclamation at a later stage. Our aim as Christians is that we should, together with Muslims, learn to recognize God's action in history and God's purpose for the present. We are not unconcerned with each other's contribution; we are not in mutually exclusive competition. At some points we are in tension with each other and it is our desire that we may learn to make this a constructive tension. Paradox is almost always necessary for a grasp upon truth. We learn in order to serve each other and in order that we may both serve our fellow men.

DIALOGUE FOR SERVICE

Many Christians work alongside Muslims in industrial, medical, and educational fields in Britain today. Each needs to win the other's confidence to further their cooperation with each other. A Muslim will be quick to recognize the Christian who genuinely desires the spiritual and physical well-being of Muslims as Muslims. A Christian should graciously and gratefully accept the service of a Muslim.

Everyone is called to cooperate in meeting the needs of individuals and in sharing the rebuilding of society. It is often the laymen who already meet across religious frontiers at their everyday work in offices and factories, in village life, in educational institutions and in hospitals. They are already involved in working together and they look for guidance to avoid the misunderstandings or obstructions which may be caused by religious differences. It is no longer only in secular institutions that Christians and Muslims and secularists are colleagues. It happens that Muslims work in Christian institutions and that Muslim institutions receive Christian colleagues. Many Christian mission hospitals train and employ Muslim staff. I have known a Christian who worked to train Qur'an readers in Nigeria to become fully qualified teachers.

At Selly Oak colleges, as well as learning about Muslims, students are anxious to help Muslims. Many Muslim immigrants in our city of Birmingham are lonely, or they need help with learning English, or with adjustment to British social patterns. Students who are teachers or nurses may offer their professional and voluntary skills to helping these immigrants. They are not trying to extract them from their previous roots; integration is not a one-sided absorbing of newcomers, but it is a mutual awareness of each other's traditions and a collaboration in serving each other and society in general. In order to promote such mutuality other Christian workers in schools, hospitals, and government offices have given up their weekends or evenings to attend courses in the religious background of immigrants whom they wish to know and serve better.

Muslims and Christians can be united in their sense of responsibility to the secularized but not necessarily secularist world. Neither religious tradition regards theological speculation, symbolic expression, or ritual performance as self-contained spiritual exercises. The ethic of the Qur'an insists upon the service of man to man as individuals, and of men to men as communities. The Qur'an speaks of a religion of this world as well as a religion of the next world. Christians recall Jesus' prayer that they are not taken out of this world, but sent into it. This implies participation in the secular concerns of the modern world. It is emphatically not a question of a religious pact against the process of secularization or even the ideology of secularism. It is a belief that religious men's vision and dedication extend to all areas of human need, and this must be a challenge to any secularist or humanist claim to have found all the answers!

The practical claims of both Muslim and Christian traditions urge upon both the need for planning more effective collaboration in education, in social welfare, in charitable giving. The Qur'anic teaching concerning almsgiving and the subsequent Muslim institution which expresses that teaching show these noble principles of men serving God by the service of their fellow men. If an institution is neglected, the values behind it may be lost; the institution of charitable almsgiving, however it is implemented, reformed, or resuscitated, is primarily an expression of Qur'anic values of human compassion of communal interdependence and individual responsibility for this to God.

DIALOGUE . . . WITH GOD?

Learning and service may be ways of cooperation where Muslims and Christians may grow closer together. The chief justification for our encounter and dialogue is that it may lead us closer to responding to God's dialogue with men. It is the glorious experience of both Muslims and Christians that God has spoken to men in history and that God has heeded men's prayers to him.

Let us briefly examine a central theme which could be a mutually enriching theme for dialogue—the concept of revelation. The Muslims' belief that God has revealed his Word in the sending down (*tanzil*) of the Qur'an is, for them, the central point of Divine revelation. For Christians this central point is God's revelation of himself in the Word made flesh. For the Muslim the Qur'an is unique and beyond imitation; for the Christian Jesus Christ is unique and beyond comparison. Neither Jesus nor the Qur'an claim to invalidate previous prophecy where man heard God's speaking. Even though God speaks and acts in history, his Word is eternal, for both Muslims and Christians. This eternity gives it a freshness which each man must hear anew for himself; as historians and semanticists we must listen with the ears of the first century A.D. or A.H., but as worshippers we must listen with ears that are not deafened by but not deaf to the clamour of our own century.

We respond to him when we hear him; some of us claim to hear him more clearly in the Qur'an, some of us claim to hear him more fully in Christ. We cannot close our eyes to these radical differences of priority. Yet this does not exclude our search for common ground, on the basis of which we shall be better equipped to tackle those differences. However, our claims that the Qur'an is inimitable, and that Christ is incomparable are not necessarily mutually exclusive or antagonistic. The Muslim looks back to see that the Qur'an is not discontinuous with previous prophecy (Qur'an: 98.2). The Christian looks back too, to see the many and various ways in which God has spoken (Heb. 1.1) and that God never left himself without a witness (Acts 14.17). For both Christian and Muslim a doctrine of particularist, special revelation must be set in the context of general revelation, the signs of God the Creator's love for all.

The difference of our response may obscure the fact that we have faith given to us by the one God. The first article of both Christians' and Muslims' creeds is faith in the one God. I use the word "God" for both. If I were an Arab Christian speaking Arabic, I should say "Allah" for both. But I am speaking English and use "God". To make a distinction would be dualism or polytheism. It is the wonder and mystery of his revelation of his Word that should focus our attention together on to a path which seeks not our own glorification but his. In dialogue on a spiritual level we are not so much concerned with our own traditional channels of response as with our present and future relationship with God as he reveals himself to us. If we show love and patience to each other and if we covet that which is best for our fellow men, then we are more likely to discover God's love for us, his patience with us, and his purpose for the well-being of all his creation.

We need some spiritual expression for our dialogue together and for our dialogue with God. We need to pray more regularly *for* each other. We need a greater sense of praying *with* each other. In some places reverent experimentation has been made with inter-faith services with men of other religious traditions. These may have been occasions of festival, of celebration, of hospitality, or of silent penitence. There can be great enrichment in attentive openness to each other's scriptures; the Christian may come to feel the impact of the Qur'an's teaching, the Muslim may come to feel the example of Christ's life. There have been times for joint intercessions, as when Muslim nurses in Indonesia invite Christians to pray with them for their patients, or as when Christian teachers in England have found ways of drawing Muslim children into non-confessional patterns of worship.

When we use the words "Muslim" or "Christian", we should be essentially describing a relationship with God—a relationship of submission to the gift of faith and to the gift of grace. And yet, we so often use the words as labels, as communal descriptions. This is not to suggest that communal loyalties are unimportant; but the Islamic *Ummah* and the Church are made up of individuals committed to God. Sometimes we are too anxious to define the frontiers of our community, so that both Muslims and Christians lose their universalist and eschatological horizons. Could a Muslim regard a Christian as a man of faith, a *mu'min*, and a man who submits himself to God, a *muslim* (with a small "m")? Could a Christian regard a Muslim as Christ-like in his obedience to God and in his service to men? If we could accord this spiritual recognition to each other and could meet together in the spirit of prayer, we might well avoid the hypocrisy, self-sufficiency, and spiritual pride which both the Qur'an and Jesus Christ so forcibly denounce.

As Muslims and Christians we should not be owing our chief loyalty to any false absolutes of power or of communal interests or of human religious traditions. This can be a form of idolatry.

We can both share the great cry of worship—"God is greater", *Allahu akbar*. Perhaps there can be nothing more compulsive than this adoration of the larger, mysterious (but not mystifying) God to urge deeper understanding, more patient and more practical dialogue—in the academic world, in the secular world in our religious life.

God *is* greater, and to his judgement we offer our submission, *islam*, and our love. Whatever we learn in our dialogue, whatever we communicate with each other, whatever we transmit to this world, all is in the context of the Last Day. "Our knowledge and our prophecy alike are partial, and the partial vanishes when wholeness comes . . . My knowledge now is partial; then it will be whole, like God's knowledge of me" (1 Cor. 13.9 and 12).

DIALOGUE . . . IN THE WORLD?

Religious values are becoming more and not less necessary in many parts of the world to challenge at the deepest level complacency over material inequalities, to provoke compassion for vast suffering, to bring reconciliation and non-violent resolution to obdurate racial tensions. It is especially urgent that religion be reconciling rather than divisive when one recalls how religion may be misused within situations of tension, and how it may be distorted into self-righteousness and prejudice. In the Christian–Muslim context one thinks again sadly of dangers in Ethiopia, the Sudan, Nigeria, the Middle East, Birmingham and Bradford—and our whole tragic history of mutual enmity summarized in the blasphemous enterprise of the Crusades.

If the freedom through the Spirit of God is truly our inheritance of salvation (cf. 2 Cor. 3.17) then this must be a responsible freedom whereby we participate, not in a static or utopian plan, but in the dynamic and eternal purpose of God for the world. If we have this incarnational, universal, and eschatological frame of reference we shall be given new optimism, and new patience. In the still almost untouched areas of inter-religious understanding, co-operation, and witness to God, we shall find a new way to serve our fellow men and to glorify God. We shall find God's forgiveness for our past arrogance and ignorance, instead of brooding over them impenitently, resentfully, or despairingly. In our present inter-religious tensions we shall find strength to win reconciliation with each other, with the world, and with God. In our faith for the future we shall submit our purpose to God's purpose, not presuming to know all his mind, but grateful whenever he reveals it to us.

It is perhaps a hard criterion that I have chosen to test the relevance of religious world-views in the modern world. I believe that religious man must demonstrate in an ideologically and religiously pluralistic world that his world-view is not fragmenting and fatalist, but uniting and purposive, liberating and responsible. Man's prerogative or "privilege" is as God's servant or son, and here I reject any invidious suggestion that there is for Christians a necessary and complete contradiction between man's servanthood and man's sonship. We are free because we have been freed, we are rich because we are indebted, we are strong because we are enabled; as sons and as brothers we always owe duty and love to him whom we know as our Father. In face of the apparently overwhelming problems and the staggering opportunities which technology raises, we believe that religious world-views can set moral, social, and individual priorities and can radically challenge and displace men's false absolutes, restricted time-scales, and irresponsible selfishness.

Can our inter-religious coexistence become inter-religious co-operation where we work with each other and with God? Can our inter-religious confrontation become inter-religious communion, as we converse together and listen for God's converse with us? Can our inter-religious witness suspend the judgement (which is God's prerogative) and point each other and our fellow men not to ourselves but to God? Can such living, working, and speaking together (and, for some of us, our waiting upon God in prayer together) exemplify a new relevance for religious values, for religious responsibility, for religious truth, amid the great problems and the still greater opportunities of the modern age?

Only thus can our religious world-views demonstrate the freedom of the Spirit. Only thus will our responsibility become commitment to and co-operation in God's purpose, where our sickness can be overcome by God's grace.

FOR FURTHER READING

K. CRAGG, *Christianity in World Perspective*. 1968.

C. F. HALLENCREUTZ, *New Approaches to Men of Other Faiths*. Geneva, W.C.C. 1970.

N. SMART, *World Religions: A Dialogue*. 1960, 1966.

W. C. SMITH, *Questions of Religious Truth*. 1967.

7

The Theology of Mission

Douglas Webster

Mission is first and last about God. He initiates it; he completes it. God is always the subject of mission. There is a theology of mission only because Christian theology is essentially missionary. Mission is not an item of theology, one among others. There would be no theology apart from the divine mission of our missionary God. There is a sense therefore in which mission precedes theology and accounts for it. God's mission creates theology. Mission is a dimension of theology as it is a dimension of prayer and of life itself.

Mission presupposes both the sickness of man and the salvation of God. The very vagueness of our belief in God is not merely a symptom of our sickness, it is the root of our disease. The contemporary crisis in the understanding of mission is basically an outcome of the contemporary crisis in the debate about God. David Jenkins began one of his public lectures with these words: "I suspect that there is nothing much wrong with God. A great deal of the Church and a very great deal of theology would seem, however, to be in a pretty sickly condition." (David Jenkins: *Living with Questions*, 1969, p. 58.) At the present time we see this sickness focused in the World Council of Churches. We may hope that its nadir was reached at the Uppsala Assembly in 1968. There are some theological statements in the Uppsala Report on mission, but what was produced was far more a sociology of mission than a theology of mission. At Uppsala mission appears to be determined more by the nature of man than by the nature of God. Yet if mission becomes divorced from theology and increasingly secularized, the future of Christianity is at stake. There can be no Christian mission apart from theology, and all theology is ultimately missionary and has missionary effects.

Like the gospel itself, mission also suffers constantly from being misunderstood. It is inevitably an insult to man in his *hubris*, more than ever now that he claims to have come of age. Mission is part of the foolishness of God; it affronts the wisdom of man. Indifference to mission and its secularization is part of the very different foolishness of the Church; it saves the Church from the Cross. That is why I have said that mission presupposes both the sickness of man and the salvation of God. I invite you to approach the theology of mission in terms of sickness and salvation.

Consider these words of Jesus:

> I have come that men may have life, and may have it in all its fullness . . . the Son of Man has come to seek and to save what is lost. . . . It is not the healthy that need a doctor, but the sick. . . . I did not come to invite virtuous people, but sinners. . . . It is for judgement that I have come into this world—to give sight to the sightless and to make blind those who see. . . . The Son of Man did not come to be served but to serve, and to surrender his life as a ransom for many. . . . He came to his own home, and his own people received him not [RSV]. . . . The light has come into the world, but men preferred darkness to light because their deeds were evil. . . . I have come accredited by my Father, and you have no welcome for me; if another comes self-accredited you will welcome him . . . I have not come of my own accord. I was sent by one who truly is, and him you do not know. . . . I have come into the world as light, so that no one who has faith in me should remain in darkness. . . . My task is to bear witness to the truth. For this was I born; for this I came into the world, and all who are not deaf to truth listen to my voice.[1]

In all these sayings we have an impressive, but not exhaustive, selection of statements by Jesus about his mission, what brought it about, what it was intended to accomplish. Implicitly or explicitly, they all describe the human situation as sickness and

[1] All these quotations, except the one noted, are from the New English Bible.

the divine purpose as salvation. Each of those statements concerns his coming into the world and the reason for it. All verses in the New Testament which refer either to the coming of Christ or the sending of Christ relate to his mission. So the theology of mission must include both a theology of sickness and a theology of salvation.

It is no exaggeration to say that when its theology of mission is weak the Church itself is weak. The churches that are strong are not necessarily those with the most members or the best income, or those which enjoy privilege of one kind or another. Strong churches are generally those whose missionary obedience is deep. Mission is more than the activism of doing good or protesting against injustice. Mission is more than aid, more than service, more than open-ended discussion. The great problems of our day are world poverty and race hatred. The two are related. They provide the context of mission. Any engagement in mission which ignores either of these vast issues is totally irrelevant. But although they give the context of mission, they do not determine the content of mission or its goal. Mission is more than feeding the hungry, though to feed the hungry is an important part of loving our neighbour. Mission is more than breaking down racial and colour prejudice, though doing this is an imperative part of Christian witness. At Uppsala it seemed to be implied that mission was entirely determined and measured by these great issues. That is not so. In the last analysis mission is concerned only, ultimately, supremely with God. The gospel is about God. Man does need bread; man does need dignity; but above all man needs God. St Peter gives his own summary of Christ's mission: "Christ also died for our sins once and for all. He, the just, suffered for the unjust, *to bring us to God.*" From the Christian viewpoint, being poor, being deprived, being oppressed, are serious misfortunes which the gospel is meant to remedy. But they are not final disasters. In the biblical perspective sin matters more than poverty and guilt more than hunger. Christ was more concerned for the fate of the rich man who lost his soul than for the beggar who rested on Abraham's bosom. Because so much contemporary thinking about mission—it cannot be called theology—centres on poverty or non-whiteness instead of the sickness of mankind, rich and poor alike, we have departed from New Testament views.

This was the wrong turning taken at Uppsala. The human tragedy was seen as hunger, not as sin. The worst privation was racial inequality, not ignorance of God. Yet the slave plantations produced the negro spirituals, whereas the affluence of California has produced Satanism and the drug scene. Slavery was a terrible evil and eventually the Church took its part in wiping it out. But it was not a worse evil than the moral slavery of the affluent society. Jesus affirmed that "it is easier for a camel to go through the eye of a needle than for a rich man to enter the kingdom of God". By the same token it is better to be a slave working on a sugar plantation or a black man in a South African gaol, knowing Christ, than to be a slave-owner or a member of the South African government, not knowing Christ. It was Jesus himself who said: "How blest are you who are poor; the kingdom of God is yours. How blest are you who now go hungry; your hunger shall be satisfied." He saw that the real issues were not economic but spiritual. This is where Christianity stands over against Marxism. I am not for one moment defending or excusing poverty, hunger, or racism. Our Christian calling is to fight against the lot. But I do question any theology of mission which sees ultimate human need in terms of poverty rather than in terms of godlessness. The heresy of Uppsala was not its concern with poverty and race, for every Christian ought to be concerned with these things. Its heresy was the diversion of missionary attention almost exclusively into these channels instead of addressing it to the whole world, whether rich or poor, white or coloured, who know nothing of the God and Father of our Lord Jesus Christ. In the Bible the most serious element in the human situation is not poverty but unbelief. The basic sickness is not economic or social or political: it is moral, it is sin. Jesus sends the Holy Spirit to "convince the world of sin . . . because they do not believe in me" (John 16.8, 9 RSV); and to the Jews he said "If you do not believe that I am what I am, you will die in your sins" (John 8.24). Uppsala treated poverty far more seriously than unbelief or sin, and so its theology of mission became distorted from the proclamation of God's saving action to the service of human need.

In the Gospel narratives Jesus shows much more concern with the sick than with the poor. He himself was poor. He did not regard the poor as in spiritual peril. It was those who made people

poor and kept them poor who were in peril. He did not regard
being oppressed as the ultimate evil; being the oppressor was far
worse. Sickness was not suffering from oppression or colonialism
or injustice or cruelty, but being responsible for these things,
condoning them, perpetrating them. Uppsala was right up to a
point, in that it insisted that mission should be addressed to the
power structures of modern society; it was right in recognizing
that "centres of power control human life for good and evil"
(Uppsala Report, p. 30). But its grappling with evil was insufficient
and shallow. There is evil in the structures because there is evil
in men. Structures are not necessarily evil, but the biblical view of
humanity, which Jesus endorsed, is that "the whole head is sick,
and the whole heart faint" (Isa. 1.5 RSV). Uppsala saw clearly the
evil in war, racism, world poverty; it failed to see evil, as the
Bible does, in the whole human race. It pinpointed the visible
warts and horrible blemishes on the *corpus humanum*; it paid
little attention to the sin, the spiritual alienation, which is the
fundamental sickness. And this is characteristic of a great deal
that goes today for a theology of mission.

To say that evil infects the whole human race is not to say that
man is totally evil. The reading of literature, history, or the
Bible forbids any such conclusion. We can be appalled at the
crimes and brutality of Stalin, just as his daughter was, but her
Twenty Letters to a Friend show tenderness and love even in a man
who did great evil. Man's sickness is not merely his sin: it is his
torn-apartness, the conflicts and contradictions that make him
what he is, that make us what we are. David Jenkins describes
the story of the Fall as "that cameo of the human situation which
links together the contradictoriness of the human situation as we
experience it with the much broader and more decisive Old
Testament statement that human existence is part of a creation
which is good and which is intended to fulfil good ends" (*What
is Man?*, p. 81). Man can collaborate with God in his creative
work and at the same time he can resist God and destroy both
himself and God's work. Our present awareness of the problems
and dangers of our environment illustrates this, quite apart from
Genesis 3. Man's vocation is to exercise dominion over the
environment. His sickness is that he either dominates in a harm-
ful and destructive way or else allows the environment to domi-
nate him. Philip Mason's important book, *Patterns of Dominance*,

examines this in respect of race. At the beginning he mentions
"the lifelong habit of dependence which has made so many of
mankind unfit for freedom, truly slaves by nature" (p. 13). At
the end, writing of the desirable society, he points out that

> man has the techniques, if he will use them, which would
> enable him to grow more food than he does and to limit his
> numbers to what he can feed, to live in peace and justice.
> What hinders him is himself, his own fear, greed, and jealousy.
> It is unlikely that there will ever be human creatures on earth
> free from these passions; personal life is centred on the ego,
> social life on the group. But the art of living in society is to
> devise means of harnessing and training this unruly selfhood,
> of making it easier to live in amity with our neighbours.
> There are good reasons for supposing it will become more
> difficult rather than less.[1]

The whole of David Anderson's fascinating book *The Tragic
Protest*, which he sub-titles "A Christian study of some modern
literature", explores the sickness of man as portrayed in contemporary novels, mostly by those who would not claim to be
Christians in any sense at all. One chapter, dealing with existentialist authors such as Jean-Paul Sartre, he calls "Man at Absolute
Zero". For Sartre "this is the challenge with which twentieth-
century man is faced: to create his own meanings within a meaningless universe, to start from *absolute zero*" (p. 35). The difference
between Sartre and Jesus is that "Sartre believes that such a life
can be self-generated, whereas Jesus believed it could come only if
a man opened himself up to the will of God" (p. 42). He remarks
later that "in Sartre, everything seems to go bad on us—even
what is highest and best in man becomes deformed and trivial-
ized. The exceeding sinfulness of sin has seldom been more
relentlessly exposed by one writer" (p. 63). Discussing Kafka he
suggests that "modern man is like a river which has overflowed its
banks. He has pushed his inquiries too far, like a river which,
forgetting its own proper limits, has lost its outline and shape
and tries to ignore its destiny by forming little seas in the interior
of the land" (p. 117). Kafka exhibited despair, and in his despair
he set up warning signs. "We have eaten of the tree of knowledge: now we must eat of the tree of life" (p. 123).

[1] Philip Mason, *Patterns of Dominance* (O.U.P. 1970), pp. 339f.

Is it not curious, even ironical, that while large sections of the Church, as exemplified at Uppsala and elsewhere, pay scant attention to the problem of sin and man's moral and spiritual sickness, from right outside the Church we have such penetrating diagnosis and affirmations of it? Uppsala was indeed concerned with certain evils, but very selective in its choice of them. The World Council of Churches continues to point out the sins and the sickness and the guilt of the West—quite rightly. It would be taken more seriously, however, if it were more impartial and occasionally showed a like concern and disapproval for the evils of Russia and the communist bloc and the many sicknesses in those lands which make up the so-called third world. *Apartheid* is indeed a loathsome evil, but Africa has other evils also and most of them are much older and some of them are much worse in their effects on the community. It is the demonic element in the world which is being forgotten. What are we to make of such words as St John's: "the whole godless world lies in the power of the evil one" (1 John 5.19)? This theme of evil receives profound treatment in the fourth Gospel but scarcely gains a mention in modern theological writing about mission, quite apart from Uppsala. Men still sin when they come of age; the difference is that their sin is more responsible and therefore more tragic. It is hardly necessary for me to cite examples of our contemporary sickness. It is commonplace to speak of sick humour or the sick joke; there is sick art; society itself is sick. St Paul said that Christ Jesus came into the world to save sinners. His mission was to the sick. In biblical theology this is not a category of humanity: it is humanity itself, all of it without exception. How strange it is that in our generation poets and novelists with no particular Christian affiliations should have to remind us of the grave sickness of man which the Church seems largely to have forgotten! Modern literature takes evil more seriously than modern theology. We may well find more of a rationale for mission in the literature of our day than in its theology. Pornography and horror stories cry out with anguish for the catharsis of the Holy Redeemer. They ache for the saving word, the healing touch, the authoritative pardon and release.

My first point then is that the theology of mission arises from the Christian doctrine of man and the phenomenon of sickness. The sickness can be physical, social, economic, moral, spiritual.

They that are whole have no need of a physician, but they that are sick. Jesus was not implying that some people needed him and others did not. He was saying that some people recognized their need and others were blind to it. The divine mission is validated not by human recognition but by human need, the need to be perfect as the heavenly Father is perfect. "I am the Lord your God . . . be holy, for I am holy" (Matt. 5.48; Lev. 11.44). The purpose of the divine mission is the recovery of man's defaced divine image, that man should become holy and therefore whole.

My second point derives from the Christian doctrine of God and the phenomenon of salvation. This is the great theme of the New Testament and it is the heart of the gospel. The verb "to save" and the noun "salvation" together appear no less than 150 times in the New Testament. Basically each is connected with the idea of health. Salvation means the restoration of health to one who has lost it, to restore safety to one who is threatened by danger, to snatch from death someone who is about to perish (J–J. von Allmen: *Vocabulary of the Bible*, pp. 384 f.). Jesus is the author and pioneer of our salvation. The Gospel tells of a historical salvation achieved for mankind by Jesus Christ in his life, death, and resurrection. He saved others, himself he could not save. The salvation which Jesus brings is not temporary and provisional but total and ultimate; the noun is often used in an absolute sense. Those who put their faith in Christ enter upon the way of salvation. This salvation was regarded by New Testament Christians as a present experience. Paul refers to "us who are being saved" (1 Cor. 1.18 RSV). Salvation is not so much a possession as a sphere in which we are called and enabled to live. The Gospel itself "is the saving power of God for everyone who has faith" (Rom. 1.16). But although this salvation can be experienced as an immediate reality, it has a future aspect and manifestation. "We await a Saviour, the Lord Jesus Christ," says Paul (Phil. 3.20 RSV). "Salvation is nearer to us now than when we first believed" (Rom. 13.11 RSV). So while it is a past event and a present experience, there is a further apprehension of it which is still in the future.

Jesus himself uses the language of salvation and it is synonymous with the language of healing. To a forgiven woman he could say "Your faith has saved you" and to a blind man whose sight he had restored, "Your faith has cured you" (Luke 7.50; 18.42),

using the same word on each occasion. The forgiveness of sins
and the healing of the paralytic are identical: one pronouncement
achieved both.

There is a natural tendency for each generation to see different
things in Jesus and to emphasize one or other aspect of his
character. In the 1920s and 1930s Christian leaders such as Charles
Raven and Dick Sheppard saw him as a pacifist. Today many
radicals see him as the revolutionary, the awakener of guerillas.
It is always dangerous to use Christ to authenticate our own
views. But there can be no doubt whatever that in the New
Testament and through the early Christian centuries he was seen
supremely as the Saviour. The whole of the New Testament is
written round this idea. The availability of full salvation was the
good news of the gospel. The inescapable desire to share this
good news with other people is what made the Church missionary from the outset.

Of the four evangelists it is Luke who most firmly sets his
gospel in this framework of salvation. He begins his birth narrative with a reference to Caesar Augustus whom Virgil had
celebrated as "the one who has been promised again and again".
The official faith of the empire was that Augustus was the world's
saviour. He was still reigning when Jesus was born. The Augustan
age was golden, but "even the great Augustus could only bind,
not conquer, the demons of history" (E. Stauffer: *Christ and the
Caesars*, p. 100). When Luke wrote, Augustus and many of his
"divine" successors had died. Jerusalem had fallen. And he
records the obscure birth of a Jewish boy accompanied by angelic
songs which hailed the advent of a Saviour in the city of David.
The three songs which Luke inserts and the Church still sings
all acclaim the arrival of salvation. Mary rejoices in "God my
Saviour" and relates the effects of his saving deed. Zechariah
blesses God "for he has visited and redeemed his people, and has
raised up a horn of salvation for us in the house of his servant
David". He expands the meaning of that deliverance. Simeon,
with the child in his arms, sings contentedly "mine eyes have
seen thy salvation". In chapter 4 Luke puts the opening of the
Lord's ministry in the Nazareth synagogue with a sermon on a
text from Isaiah about the meaning of salvation. In that brief
passage he quoted we have the verb to proclaim twice and the
verb to preach good news once. At the end of his gospel the

Lord's last words to his disciples are: "Thus it is written, that the Christ should suffer and on the third day rise from the dead, and that repentance and forgiveness of sins should be preached in his Name to all nations" (Luke 24.46 f.).

Here is ample material for a theology of mission which is at one and the same time a theology of salvation. The essential thing about this kind of salvation is that it should be proclaimed. We find the apostles doing just this in the Acts. They are quite uncompromising. They want everyone within reach to know what God has done in Jesus Christ. They are prepared to go to prison for preaching him as the Saviour and Lord of all. They want other people to become Christians, to join the saved and saving community and be in the way of salvation. They are emphatic that "there is no salvation in anyone else at all, for there is no other name under heaven granted to men, by which we may receive salvation" (Acts 4.12).

This confronts us with one of the great debates today in all thinking about the theology of mission. No satisfactory conclusion was reached at Uppsala—indeed the main issues were entirely dodged. The Church must really ask itself whether it still believes all this. Have we outgrown it? Did the apostolic age make a false start? Has the concept of salvation become meaningless? Should we openly depart from the central theme of the New Testament and honestly admit what we are doing and why? Ought the Church now to concentrate on other forms of mission and quietly forget the scandalous event that brought it into being and the scandalous preaching of its early days? Can we have a theology of mission without a theology of salvation? Can there be mission without a gospel of salvation? On the answers to questions like these the future of Christianity and its place in the world for the next few decades may well depend. I sincerely believe it to be the greatest issue facing not merely the missionary movement but all the Churches and especially the World Council of Churches. For if we no longer believe in salvation we have no gospel and no reason for engaging in mission, at least in that aspect of it which is called evangelism. Bishop Stephen Neill in a recent article has posed this quite bluntly, "If we put the plain question, 'Do you want people to be converted?', from many of our contemporary ecumenical theologians the answer will be a resounding 'No'. If we are evangelicals, must not the answer be a resounding 'Yes'?" A great many catholics would, of course, rank with evangelicals in this matter, as would a substantial number of the orthodox.

Let us examine briefly what these two possible answers mean. If it is not right to want people to be converted to Christ, Christians who hold this view are making certain assumptions. Either they deny the root sickness of humanity and are at heart humanists, or they deny the reality of or the necessity for that salvation which caused the New Testament to be written; or they think that there are other ways of salvation apart from Jesus Christ. We have seen good reason for taking seriously the phenomenon of sickness. We have had to conclude that the New Testament cannot be explained except by the fact that something happened which brought into the reach of man an experience called salvation; the evidence for this alone could have more than filled this chapter. We have also noticed that, rightly or wrongly, the first Christians firmly believed that this salvation was to be found nowhere except in Christ. If even the Judaism which had produced the Christ failed to provide an adequate way of salvation, so that the first Christians had to leave the synagogue or were driven from it, *a fortiori* the New Testament does not allow for a way of salvation in any other religion apart from Christ.

In order to forestall misunderstanding, let it be clear that we are ascribing salvation to Christ, not to the institutional Church which had barely come into existence. We are not saying that Christ is confined to his Church. We are not denying the possibility of ultimate salvation to the adherents of other religions or to the millions who live and die with no knowledge of Jesus Christ. A God who allowed the eternal destiny of his children to depend on accidents of history and contingencies of birth, culture, geography, and race, would be very different from the God whom Jesus addressed as Father. We know it is the will of God that "all men should find salvation and come to the knowledge of the truth" (1 Tim. 2.4). If this is his will we cannot believe that he puts obstacles in his own way. On the contrary, in Christ he removed the obstacles and the misconceptions about his means of salvation. What the New Testament asserts is that whether inside or outside the Church, whether in this life or the next, God's salvation is through Christ and in Christ alone. We are not obliged to dismiss the great religions of the world as false or

valueless; few theologians would take such a course today. Most
religions have their theology of salvation and it is very different
from the Christian Gospel. In so far as they are concerned with
truth, other religions will point men in the direction of the true
God, and those who are genuinely seeking truth must eventually
encounter one who claimed to be the way, the truth, and the life.
Because Christian theology is convinced that the truth overcomes
the lie and that God's truth is in Jesus, it need not be aggressive
in its approach to those of other faiths nor arrogant in presenting
the one who would not break a bruised reed nor quench the
smoking flax. It quietly and gladly proclaims that there is only one
Saviour and only one salvation. Not to believe this would dis-
pense us from any desire that other people should become
Christians and any attempt to help them to become Christians.
Conversion would be abhorrent. But the logic of believing this
projects the believer into mission, for failure to share with others
the supreme wonder and the gift beyond words runs the risk of
forfeiting it altogether. The first Christian generation were irre-
pressible. "We cannot possibly give up speaking of things we
have seen and heard", said the apostles in court. And the things
they had seen and heard were about salvation; and the reason why
they were in court was that through them the risen Christ had
healed a man lame from birth—he had been saved—and they had
used this incident as a visual aid to the new salvation which they
proclaimed with such courage and determination.

Perhaps we may find a useful analogy in scientific and particularly medical research. There is a marvellous instinct in man to
conquer pain and disease, and the history of medicine records one
triumph after another. Many a malady which once killed kills no
longer. People can be saved from malaria, tuberculosis, leprosy,
and much more. The way of healing has been discovered. Most
discoveries are made by a lonely research scientist or a team
working in a laboratory. When their work is completed and the
experiments successful, the news that one more affliction has been
cured is publicized. If the research men kept their knowledge
secret the practitioners could not use it. But science has been
magnificently generous. New knowledge is made known at the
earliest possible moment and made available round the world. It is
proclaimed. So it has been with the Gospel. It is addressed to
depths of sickness far beyond natural medicine. Jesus Christ has

Dcc

saved those who were written off as helpless or incurable or irreformable. He has been doing this in every century and for the last two hundred years in every continent. If a new drug for some physical ailment is worth proclaiming on a world scale, displacing superstitious or ineffective remedies, are we at this stage in Christian history to cease proclaiming the salvation that is in Christ?

Yet this is the major issue in the theology of mission today— it is the nub of the debate. There are those who would abolish all such proclamation and would advocate giving up every attempt to evangelize or make converts. They would urge that proclamation must now give way to service on the one hand and dialogue on the other. Both these are valid modes of mission. There are many situations where proclamation would be utterly ineffective except after countless acts of service which elicit the questions that enable proclamation to have meaning. There are many situations where any brash and insensitive proclamation of the gospel would defeat its own object; the history of mission is littered with the casualties this has produced. No intelligent Christian concerned with mission today is likely to doubt the crucial importance of both service and dialogue. In the citadels of other faiths there has been nothing like enough of either. Infinite harm can be done by too much proclamation and by too much speaking of any kind, just as some kinds of commercial advertising are counter-productive and create sales resistance to those who weary of the same old slogans. Television commercials should at least have taught the Church this. But by this argument I am not pleading for excess. I am urging that a halt should be called to negative attitudes to mission which would empty it of its central task and glory, that of telling to every generation and every society what God has done in Christ for the salvation of the whole human race.

The techniques of proclamation are another matter and outside the scope of a discussion on the theology of mission. Proclamation is not monologue; it is not limited to sermons; it does not preclude discussion—at its best it invites it. There can be a certain kind of proclamation within a dialogue; service itself may sometimes be a form of proclamation. All this may be granted. Love can be expressed in words and in deeds. Most people use and want both. The words without deeds can fail to convince; the deeds without words can fail to satisfy. So it is with proclamation. Jesus fed the hungry. He also spoke to them about the bread of life. He told his friends that his death was connected with their sins. He also took bread and broke it and asked them to drink from a common cup of the New Covenant. He washed their feet. He told them what it meant in words. His whole ministry was a masterly knitting together of deeds and words, signs and their interpretation. At the ultimate point deed and word blended into one, for the deed of the Cross was seen by the apostles to be the word of the Cross. The Cross spoke. At his birth the Word had become deed, the Logos was made flesh. Proclamation, therefore, is to be thought of in word and deed. Too often in the past it has been limited to words. Today the tendency is to limit it to deeds. Neither exclusively will do. Jesus did not merely talk about salvation; he made men whole.

Here then are some ingredients for a theology of mission. I have deliberately limited this essay to an approach along the two themes of human sickness and God's salvation. There is much more to be said about the theology of mission, and some of it I have tried to say elsewhere. But almost all the other items in the theology of mission relate either to a recognition of man's sickness or to the proclamation of God's salvation. It is because the prevailing theology sits lightly to both that their reconsideration is called for. No one with any perception or knowledge of the human situation can avoid weighing up the biblical analysis of its sickness. And if the Church is to remain faithful to her origins and her gospel, no one can doubt that this involves testimony to God's saving action. Ethelbert Stauffer once wrote: "The Saviour has come. He has fulfilled his great work. But he waits in silence, till the excited world notices him" (*Christ and the Caesars*, p. 184). This is profoundly true. He is silent. He has given his Church the task of speaking on his behalf. The excited world seldom notices him. The calling of the Church, its mission, is to draw the world's attention to the one who has come.

8

Is Prayer Still Valid?

Peter Baelz

I begin with a piece of autobiography. It comes from *Period Piece: A Cambridge Childhood*, by Gwen Raverat:[1]

> The first religious experience that I can remember is getting under the nursery table to pray that the dancing mistress might be dead before we got to the Dancing Class. I really could think of no other weapon of self-defence except prayer. Not that I believed in that much; still, perhaps it was worth trying.

> But, of course, prayer did not succeed. Prayers, at least *my* prayers, never did. So far as I can remember, none of the dancing mistresses from whom I suffered ever had so much as a cold in the head in all the time I knew them. There they always were, that scourge of the human race; and we always had to go through the whole degrading ritual, from the first March Past with its elegant bows to Miss Radcliffe, right down to the bitter end of the waltz or the lancers.

> I have sometimes wondered what would have been my reaction if the dancing mistress had fallen down dead as I came into the classroom. I suppose I should have felt rather guilty; but after all it would have been God's doing, not mine; and that He should have done such a thing at my request would have destroyed my respect for Him, once and for all.

> For the only virtue God had, to my mind, was impartiality;

[1] Faber and Faber 1952.

and so prayer itself seemed to me to be an immoral proceeding. It was as if you were trying to bribe the Judge. But . . . God simply never did what I asked him; so that on the whole I thought him incorruptible, which was just as well. There remained the possibility that prayer might work as magic. But even as magic it never succeeded. It was altogether a bad idea. After that, prayer became synonymous for me with giving up hope; if ever I prayed again, it was only as a final frenzy of despair, and was the first step towards resignation at not getting what I wanted.

Prayer, then, is useless. It simply does not work. It is one of those childish things which, on reaching maturity, we do well to put behind us. As rational beings we no longer believe in magic. There is no direct causal connection in the world as we know it between the uttering of a wish and its fulfilment. Words have no magical efficacy of their own: they break no bones. Furthermore, even if we eschew magic and argue that the arrow of prayer flies straight to God and that prayer's efficacy is grounded not in natural processes but in the over-riding activity of God, additional moral difficulties confront us while questions of empirical evidence remain.

To take the empirical evidence first, are we really convinced that there is a significant correlation between acts of petition and the occurrence of the things we pray for? Many Christians would confidently affirm that there is indeed such a correlation and would cite instances when their prayers have been answered. But how are we to establish the connection between the prayer and the answer? How can we eliminate the possibility of chance? Unpredictable things do happen, and sometimes they coincide with our deepest hopes and desires. If it is said that God, simply because he is God, *always* answers our prayers, though the answer is as likely to be negative as it is to be affirmative, then we have set the stage in such a way that no empirical verification or falsification is possible. Nothing can count in favour of the efficacy of prayer because nothing is allowed to count against it. The argument disappears into thin air and the sceptic is more sceptical than ever.

The sceptic's doubts are reinforced through moral considerations. If God answers prayers, does he not thereby become a respecter of persons? Is it just that he should come to the aid of those who appeal to him while leaving to their own devices those who, perhaps through no fault of their own, do not know that there is a God to whom they might appeal? Is a God who takes sides a God worthy of our deepest worship? When we hear of a man alleging, in support of his belief that prayer works, the fact that he always prays to God to give him an empty corner seat in the London-Manchester express and that he always gets one, we are very properly indignant when we think of the poor unfortunates who have to stand in the corridor for the whole journey. Of course, this is a caricature of true prayer, we say. God takes sides, if he may be said to take sides at all, not in the light of our selfish human preferences, but in the lights of his own all-good and all-wise purposes. Do we not qualify all our petitions with the words, "Not my will, but thy will be done"? Of course we do, but what is the point, then, of specifying our own particular desires, when there can be no question of bringing them to the notice of him "unto whom all hearts are open, all desires known, and from whom no secrets are hid"? Even if we grant that our prayers may sometimes be unselfish and accord with the will of God, it is difficult, if not impossible, to detect any consistent pattern of all-goodness and all-wisdom in the granting of the divine favour analogous to the pattern of goodness and wisdom which we can discern in a human parent's granting and refusing his own children's requests. Two equally believing Christian mothers pray for their child's recovery from a dangerous illness: why is the prayer of the one granted and the prayer of the other refused?

That there are ways of circumventing these difficulties, some more plausible than others, I do not dispute. All of them, however, draw heavily upon a far-reaching agnosticism about the ways of God with men. "God moves in a mysterious way, his wonders to perform." Nor do I dispute that such agnosticism is an inherent part of a total Christian faith. But if this agnosticism is to be contained within the wider context of faith, and if it is not to destroy faith, then faith in God and perseverance in prayer must be rooted elsewhere than in empirical considerations of the efficacy of prayer. If we begin with the question "Does prayer work", and look to the happenings of nature and of history to provide us with a clear answer, I suspect that most of us will be inclined to say that there is no convincing evidence to show that prayer does work. We must begin somewhere else. But where?

I suggest that we begin at the point at which Miss Raverat ended, with the thought of prayer as "the first step towards resignation at not getting what I wanted." We must all recognize the fact that in this world we often do not get what we want, whether our wants are selfish or unselfish, whether they are good, bad, or indifferent. Indeed there is a hard core of tragedy in human life. The deserving suffer misfortune and disaster as much as the undeserving. When the Psalmist declared that he had never seen the righteous forsaken, either he was living a very cloistered existence, or else piety had got the upper hand of honesty. Now tragedy can swiftly lead to despair—not simply disappointment at not getting what one wanted, but despair in the depths of a man's heart because the very meaning of life and the whole realm of personal being is threatened. Such radical despair undermines not merely this or that department of life but the whole of life. Everything is vanity, and there remains no good thing under the sun. Death has prevailed.

How are we to cope with the onset of radical despair? There are a number of classical answers to this question. We may try the way of philosophic detachment, of Stoic apathy. What will be, will be; but it is possible for a man to withdraw into the citadel of his own self and to determine to be unaffected by all that happens outside his control. Or we may make an energetic moral protest. Even if life is a pointless, bloody mess, "a tale told by an idiot, signifying nothing", nevertheless it lies within our power to create oases of meaning within the desert of meaninglessness and to achieve something of passing value before we too are swallowed up in death's destructive embrace. Or we may cultivate a kind of religious resignation. We may try to accept life, its glory and its grief, its laughter and its tears, the stars and the mud. Such deep acceptance does not deny the need for moral protest, nor even the need for an element of detachment; but it is more fundamental and more embracing than either. It is the utterance of a "Yes" to life in all its variegated forms.

You may feel like objecting at this point and telling me that I have been subtly but decisively moving my ground. I began with despair, passed from despair to resignation, and then somehow ended with a positive "Yes" to life. There is, however, nothing positive about being resigned. In fact, resignation is fundamentally negative, an acceptance of life because there is nothing that can be done except to accept. To the person making the high-sounding affirmation "I accept life" comes the bubble-pricking retort "There's not much alternative, is there?"

I agree with the gist of your objection. I have been moving my ground. Furthermore I shall move still further in a positive direction when we come to explore the character of Christian prayer. But the point that I wish to make at the moment is this. When we face the questions raised by the possibility of radical despair and consider the ways in which such despair might be encountered, we find that we are concerned with our basic attitude to life as a whole, whether it is withdrawal, protest, or acceptance. It is a matter of our fundamental human stance—or, rather, since the word "stance" connotes something more static than what I have in mind, our fundamental human reaction. We are concerned here not so much with this or that feature of the world in comparative isolation as with the world as a whole. And it is precisely in the context of this kind of question, I wish to suggest, that prayer is best to be understood.

Perhaps an illustration from the world of sport may help to elucidate what I have in mind. Take cricket, for example. When we play cricket we play, I hope, to win. We are delighted when we hit a six and despondent when we are clean bowled first ball. The game is a mixture of successes and failures, and maybe sometimes the series of failures looks as if it is never going to come to an end. Is the game still worth playing? Of course it is, we say; its value does not depend on our winning. Whether we win or lose makes no difference; it is the game that counts. We play to win, we want to win, we do our very best to win; but whether we win or lose, the game is worth playing for its own sake.

When it comes to the game of life, can something similar be said? We want happiness, success, and all the rest. We are elated when these come our way, saddened when they vanish out of our hands. But what is our attitude to the game as a whole? Is it a game to play for its own sake? Has it any point? Prayer, Christian prayer, is best understood as part of the lived response to these questions, for it is a creative participation in the meaning that Christians give to life in response to the God whom they acknowledge in faith. The primary question, then, is not "Does prayer work?", as if its essence could be captured in human and utilitarian categories, but "Is prayer valid?"

> If you came this way,
> Taking any route, starting from anywhere,
> At any time or at any season,
> It would always be the same: you would have to put off
> Sense and notion. You are not here to verify,
> Instruct yourself, or inform curiosity
> Or carry report. You are here to kneel
> Where prayer has been valid. And prayer is more
> Than an order of words, the conscious occupation
> Of the praying mind, or the sound of the voice praying.
> And what the dead had no speech for, when living,
> They can tell you, being dead: the communication
> Of the dead is tongued with fire beyond the language of the
>   living.
> Here, the intersection of the timeless moment
> Is England and nowhere. Never and always.[1]

If prayer is valid at all, it is valid in its own right, and not as a means to some end other than itself. To put the point paradoxically, we shall never begin to understand the use of prayer until we have come to terms with its uselessness. To say that some activity is useless is not the same thing as saying that it is valueless. No doubt playing games has its uses. If they are of an energetic kind, they contribute to physical health. But no one has really played a game until he has done it for the sheer fun of the thing. Making music and making love may have their uses, the one as a money-making career and the other as contributing to the increase of mankind. But their essential value lies within themselves and they require no further justification. So too, I suggest, it is with prayer. Like love, prayer may have its fruits; but, again like love, the essential value and validity of prayer are to be found in the whole activity of which prayer is an organic part and not in the consequences which may result from prayer.

It is a mistake to think of prayer exclusively in terms of particular acts of prayer or of particular times set aside for prayer. Not that I wish to suggest that there is no place for particular acts at particular times. Far from it. Indeed I do not see how a

[1] T. S. Eliot, *Four Quartets, Little Gidding.*

man's life can be prayerful unless he keeps times for such acts. But just as it is something more inclusive for a man to behave thoughtfully than it is for him to sit back and think—although he is unlikely to behave thoughtfully if he never sits back and thinks—so it is something more inclusive for a man to live prayerfully than it is for him to kneel and say his prayers. To use the adverb, to talk of a man living prayerfully, is to stress the fact that prayer characterizes the totality of the Christian life and not just one part of it. It denotes the style of the Christian life; it is a pervasive aspect of life lived Christianly. It is the practice of the presence of God.

Human beings, in order to become human, have to find a meaning for their lives. Where nothing matters, human life is at an end. Meaning can be found in a variety of activities which yield a variety of satisfactions. But at a deeper level meaning has to be created through a man's own decisions and efforts. The Christian believes that the thread which links his human meanings together is a thread which ties man to God. God is the ultimate reality of the world. The world is God's and it has its ultimate meaning in him. We shall discover ourselves as we discover him, and our life in the world is the divinely appointed place of our encounter. "It is he that hath made us and not we ourselves: we are his people and the sheep of his pasture." Or, as St Paul bids the Philippians: "Work out your own salvation with fear and trembling; for it is God that worketh in you, both to will and to do of his good pleasure." Furthermore, it is in Jesus Christ that the Christian sees the pattern and the goal of the divine-human venture. All things have been created through him and unto him. If Jesus is the supreme sacrament of God's self-giving to man, then as Jesus gave himself to the world and for the world, so the world too may become a sacrament of God's presence.

Through faith in the Father of our Lord Jesus Christ as the ultimate reality of all things the Christian accepts life. He accepts his own being-in-the-world from the hand of God. He says "Yes". Acceptance such as this is very different from passive resignation. It is shot through with thanksgiving, praise, and hope. It issues in penitence, self-offering, and service.

I have often been puzzled by St Paul's prescription that we should give thanks always for all things. It seems to demand too much and to discriminate too little. Surely we should occupy ourselves with other matters than singing an unending *Te Deum*. Surely there are many things in life for which it is altogether inappropriate to give God thanks. I hope that what I have already said may suggest some easing of the puzzlement. In the first place we can be thankful without all the time voicing our thanks. Thankfulness is an attitude as well as an activity, even if it is the case, as I believe it to be, that the practice of saying "Thankyou" is no bad recipe for learning to be thankful. Act and attitude interweave, and to say "Thank-you" even when one does not feel thankful may be a useful reminder and acknowledgement of the fact that gratitude is by no means out of place. Secondly, the object of thanking God for all things is not to pretend that there are not some things which we should much rather have done without. The little girl who was given a pin-cushion by her maiden aunt as a Christmas present was torn between good manners and honesty when she wrote: 'Thank you, Auntie, for the pin-cushion. I did want a pin-cushion. But not very much." Nor is it to pretend that the ills and accidents of life come direct from the hand of God, whether to try us or to punish us. Rather the object of thanking God for all things is to thank him for life as a whole; life seen in the perspective of Jesus Christ; the world seen as the object of God's creative and redemptive love; its pains borne as the travail of some new and glorious thing beyond our imagining; the cross transfigured by the light of the resurrection.

Thanksgiving—and hope. The world is still in process. Creation is not yet complete. The Christian looks to the future for the consummation of God's purposes. This is no bland optimism. The Christian is neither an optimist nor a pessimist. He is a realist. But he believes that the reality of the future, as the reality of the past and present, rests with God. The future is God's future. Therefore even in the midst of tragedy he dares to hope, and to hope against hope. Now the whole created order groans and travails. It is subjected to futility. But in spite of this futility hope is not lost, hope that has its origin and goal in God himself.

To live prayerfully then is to live one's life from God and towards God. The validity of this style of living depends on the truth of faith's apprehension of God as the One who gives ultimate meaning to the whole of life, as the Alpha and the Omega, the beginning and the end. If it is thanksgiving that characterizes the moment of such acknowledgement within the dynamic movement of faith, a moment of receptivity, it is self-offering which characterizes the moment of response. As we have already suggested when we were considering the springs of hope within the Christian life, God's purposes are not yet fulfilled. The world is still in the making. The Christian lives within the tension of the already and the not yet. God reigns, but we are to pray for the coming of his kingdom. The great prayer of thanksgiving, the eucharistic prayer, which forms the centre of the Church's central sacramental rite, and which expresses the pattern of thanksgiving and offering which is the underlying pattern of all Christian prayer, recalls the mighty acts of God in creation and redemption and at the same time looks forward to the consummation of all things through Jesus Christ in God's kingdom. So Christians are called to participate not only in the praise of God but also in the work of God. It is their vocation to be God's fellow-workers. In the words of the simple but profound vestry prayer, "Grant that we who have been with thee around thy table may continue with thee at thy work in thy world." The divine love stretches out to embrace the whole world, to feed the hungry, to release the prisoners, and to preach good tidings to the poor. Thus to pray that God's will be done on earth as it is in heaven, is to commit oneself to participation in the on-going creative and redemptive work of Christ. To live from and towards God is to live with and for our fellow-men in the world. Thanksgiving leads to offering, first and foremost the offering of ourselves, but also, because our humanity is a co-humanity which is grounded in our relationships with others, and because we are the products and in part the masters of the processes of nature, the offering of our fellow-men and of the world which together we inhabit. Such self-offering demands thought and action, but it also demands something more. If our offering is to participate in the creative and redemptive work of God, it demands exploration and discovery. We must stretch out towards the reality of the world which together we inhabit and of our fellow-men as defined and determined by the love and purposes of God. We must discover their divinely ordained potentialities. Their reality is not only what they already are but also what they are to become. To respond not only thoughtfully and responsibly, but also prayerfully, is to seek to penetrate the ambiguities and fantasies which bedevil the present and to discover the reality which is waiting to be born. It is to learn a deeper sensitivity and a true responsiveness, to pierce the veil of our own preconceptions and predilections, to see the whole of life as it is for God, to catch the breath of the Creator Spirit. It is to discern the world in God and to respond to God in the world.

Perhaps I have said enough to indicate what I mean by suggesting Christian living is prayerful living and that prayer characterizes the whole of the Christian life and not just one part of it. It is time now to look more closely at particular acts of prayer. I hope it will be obvious, however, that such acts should never be divorced from the concrete wholeness of the Christian life. Granted that prayer, in the narrower and more specific sense of the word, is different from action, different even from taking thought, it is no substitute for either. Thought, prayer, and action are moments in man's total response to God. Now one, now the other, may occupy the centre of our attention. Together they form the bond which binds man and his world to God.

Prayer—and in what follows I shall be using the word to refer to specific acts of prayer—is the conscious attention of heart, mind, and spirit to God. It is recollection and aspiration. It is a responsive receptivity.

A closer analysis of prayer as recollection and aspiration may help to clear up a misunderstanding which not unnaturally arises when we think of prayer in connection with our basic attitude to the whole of life rather than with any particular features of life, with the *that* of the world, a variegated scheme of good and evil, joy and sorrow, laughter and tears, rather than with the *how* of the world. If prayer is fundamentally a way of renewing faith, hope, and courage (you may say) is it not thereby self-regarding? Yet when we pray for someone who is going through rough waters, surely we are not just seeking to renew our own faith and hope whatever may befall that other person, keeping our own barque afloat even if his should perish beneath the waves. To make prayer intelligible in these terms is to make prayer something other than those who actually pray believe it to be. Such intelligibility is achieved at too high a cost.

In reply to this very pertinent question I wish to suggest that since prayer is self-involving a fruit of prayer will in fact be the renewal of faith, hope, and courage. Nevertheless the purpose of prayer is not to renew these positive attitudes. It is not the case that we pray in order to become more faithful, more hopeful, and

more courageous. Prayer is not a means to some end other than
itself. It is valid in its own right. It is part of our love for God, and
our love for God, just as our love for another person, is not
justified by the effects which such love has on ourselves, although
effects there will undoubtedly be. We love God because God loves
us. So, too, we pray to God, because the Spirit of God reaches
out to our own spirits.

In recollection, then, our concern is not with ourselves. It is
with God—God in himself and in and for the world. In particular
we celebrate the great facts of our creation and redemption. Since
it is in Jesus Christ that we believe that God has made himself
known to us, the words and works of Jesus, what he did and what
he suffered, offer substantial material for our meditation. So
thoughts pass into prayer and prayer into love, until, the Spirit of
God touching our own spirits, we are lost in wonder, love, and
praise. Waiting on God, receiving from God, communion with
God in a dialogue of love, spoken or unspoken, is a part of the
divine-human life to which we are called in Christ.

So, too, with confession. Here again our concern is not with
ourselves but with God. Of course, any serious confession which
is worthy of the name demands an honest self-awareness and self-
examination. But it is a mistake to imagine that in confession we
are turning our attention in upon ourselves. It is because our
attention is on God that we have to reckon with the shoddiness
and distortions of our own love. It is because we are turned in
faith and trust to God that we dare to expose ourselves to his
ruthless but merciful judgement. It is because we are drawing
near to him that we dare to seek pardon and forgiveness. He has
the will and the ability to restore the relation which we in our
ignorance and wilfulness have broken. Were our attention concentrated on our own selves, we might indeed have reason to
despair. To be over-occupied with our own sins may be a subtle
form of inverted pride. If our conscience condemn us, we do well
to remember that God is greater than our conscience. If we say
that God has indeed forgiven us but that we can never forgive
ourselves, we set the standards of our own justice above those of
the justice of God. In so doing we fail to perceive either the
extent or the cost of the divine forgiveness.

Not all our prayer is praise. Praise is the peculiar activity of
heaven. We are *in via*, not *in patria*. God seeks more than our

praise, more even than our penitence and praise. He seeks our co-operation in his work in his world. Ecclesiasticus reminds us of those whose prayer is in the work of their hands. But work, too, has its correlate in prayer, which includes aspiration as well as recollection.

In speaking of aspiration I mean that moment in prayer in which we respond to the love of God and reach out to discover his will for us in the world. The notion of discovering God's will is not as simple as it sometimes is made to sound. "How do we know what is God's will?" a simple and saintly priest was once asked. "We don't; and that's the giddy joke", came the startling reply. Certainly we have no divine blueprint for all our day-to-day decisions. Equally certainly—or perhaps I should speak only for myself—we have no hot line to heaven. But we can, taking our bearings from the person of Christ, claim to know that the divine will is one of self-giving love and that there are no limits to the divine love save only those that we place upon it ourselves. Since, then, our recognition of the divine love involves us in participation in the outpourings of divine love, our obedient and loving response to God will widen our concern, make us more sensitive to the real needs of those around us, suggest new spheres of service, new possibilities of caring. The world enters into our prayers, not only because our own being is tied up with the being of others, but because the world is God's care and concern. Before we know where we are, we are embarking on what has traditionally been called intercession. And note: such prayer does not take its origin from any magical or quasi-magical ideas of influencing God, but from the heart of Christian faith in the all-embracing and all-inclusive love of God. The image of Christ's eternal intercession in the heavenly places symbolizes this important truth. In and through him God, man, and the world are to find their ultimate harmony and perfection, and Christian prayer is part of his prayer.

As there are no limits to the divine love, so we can place no limits to the range of our intercessions. This is especially true when we are thinking of the corporate prayers of the Christian community, but even when we are thinking of our individual prayers we should remember that our prayers are part of the prayers of Christ and as such are part of the prayer of the Church, Christ's body. On the other hand, while these theological reflections seem to me valid and indisputable, and therefore provide the context within which prayer is offered and the interpretation of that prayer, and while they invite us to extend the area of our real concern where and when occasion may demand, practical considerations may well be allowed to affect the pattern and immediate concerns of our intercessions. Prayer and action are two sides of the same coin. For different people at different times they may assume different degrees of importance and urgency. The web of prayer and action within the life of the Christian community will have varying patterns. But it is not unreasonable to suppose that the individual Christian's intercessions will begin with those with whom he is or may very well be closely related. We can envisage an extending series of concentric circles, beginning with our families and friends, broadening out to include those with whom we work and play, broadening still further to embrace the community of those upon whom we depend and who depend on us, and not forgetting the fellowship of suffering, those upon whom Jesus showered his special compassion.

Again, just as we may think of varying ranges of intercession, so we may think of varying levels of intercession. A parent's concern for his child expresses itself on a number of levels. He is concerned with his physical well-being, for example, with the satisfaction of his needs and the development of his interests— that is, with his happiness—and also with his moral and spiritual growth into a mature, responsive and responsible person. So, too, in reaching out towards the divine love, and including in our prayers our searching desire and sensitive concern for the well-being of others, we may expect to find ourselves engaged at a number of different levels. Doubtless our fundamental and overriding concern will be that God may fulfil in those for whom we pray the good purpose of his perfect will. We may not know how or when this can be achieved, but this and nothing less than this is what faith and love bid us pray for. But we shall also express other levels of concern—for example, for their health and happiness. We have no reason to doubt that these represent, in one way or another, what God wills for men, even though the way that the world works, which we must believe in the end to be also the way which God chooses to work within the world which he is creating, may more or less rule out the possibility of their being achieved here and now. Once again we find the

Christian moving in the tension between the already and the not yet, and his vision and hope lead out beyond the now and the immediate future into eternity. "Thy will be done" is therefore the universal and underlying theme of our intercessions, but this will not prevent our expressing and exploring in prayer our concern with the particular and the concrete. The divine love is no distant and general benevolence; it embraces the particular as well as the universal. Was not the Word made flesh?

If intercession has its appropriate place within Christian prayer, so too has petition. Indeed it is difficult to distinguish clearly the one from the other. However, it is this element of "asking" which often causes people the greatest problems. Yet something like "asking" is an integral part of the kind of praying which I have been trying to think about. Look at it in this way. If our total response to God involves our being fellow-workers with him in the world, then our responsible activity will engage our whole personalities—our thoughts, our judgements, our decisions, and our endeavours. Linked with these are our hopes and fears, our feelings and our desires. Our actions are directed not only by our reflections and our decisions, but also by the whole complex of our inclinations, sensitivity, and discernment. What we do is determined by what we are, and what we want is very much a part of what we are. In this sense prayer is the soul's sincere desire, uttered or unexpressed. A refusal to include our own desires in our prayers is a refusal to engage with God at the deepest level of our being. Thus a merely passive "Thy will be done" is a partial withdrawal of ourselves from the presence of God, a failure to realize that God wills that in relation to him we should become more perfectly ourselves, not bloodless ghosts of ourselves. God seeks our transfiguration, not our depersonalization. The Christian emphasis is not on self-abnegation, but on losing oneself in the love of God to find oneself anew; not on dying, but on dying into life; not on selflessness, but on rebirth and resurrection. Consequently in all our aspiration we must allow our whole selves to be engaged, and we may expect our desires as well as our thoughts, our imaginations as well as our sense of duty, to be purified, transformed, and brought into obedience to the will of God. The prayer "Thy will be done" is no passive resignation, but an active wrestling with God, as the wrestling of Jacob with the angel or of Jesus in the garden of

Gethsemane. "Take this cup from me; nevertheless . . ." Acceptance is no substitute for the struggle with God; its proper place
is when the struggle is over. Is it altogether fanciful to suggest
that in this world of tragedy and disaster our honest prayer may on
occasions take the form of crying out against God, and that only
when we have cried out against him shall we learn the truth of
what it is to love and trust him? "My God, my God, why hast
thou forsaken me?" is the cry which precedes the perfect act of
self-surrender, "Into thy hands I commend my spirit." If the
psychiatrists are right in telling us that we must not be afraid to
express our anger even against those of our fellow-men whom we
love, for only in expressing it can we learn to deal with it and to
move from the threat of estrangement through reconciliation to a
new level of understanding and commitment, may not the same
be true of our relation with God? He is no headmaster jealous of
his dignity; he is the perfection of love and healing. In short, our
prayers of petition, in which we allow ourselves as we actually are
to confront the living God, ready to be re-created into what God
would have us be, are part and parcel of anything that can be
called a real relationship with the divine.

I have now said almost everything that I wish to say, and some
of my readers, I imagine, will be saying that I have not really
faced, let alone attempted to answer, the questions which really
worry them. I have said little or nothing about what actually
happens when we pray, about the effects of our prayer on the
world around us, about the things which it is all right to pray for
and the things which it is all wrong to pray for.

I must in a sense plead guilty. Certainly I do not wish to imply
that these are senseless or trivial questions. They arise. They
trouble us and they need to be answered. On the other hand the
underlying intention of everything that I have so far said has been
to suggest that they can be given a theologically satisfying answer
only if they are asked in the right context. Furthermore the right
context is not the utilitarian one of producing the goods, of asking
whether prayer works. If we begin with this question, and tackle
it along the same sort of lines as we should the question whether a
particular drug works, or whether drinking out of the far side of a
cup of water works, we shall soon find ourselves in an intellectual
morass. Neither an appeal to the testimony of others, nor a
scientifically controlled experiment, will settle the issue. The

empirical evidence is too ambiguous. What is more, even if such evidence as there is were too impressive to be swept under the carpet, there would be no necessity to appeal to the activity of God in order to account for it. There might be other naturalistic explanations which we had not yet fathomed. The right context in which to set these questions is the theological context, and it is this context which I have been trying, however unsuccessfully, to explore.

In brief, what I have said is this. Taking their starting point and direction from Jesus Christ, Christians interpret human life in the natural world as an encounter with God. The world is the object of God's creative and redemptive love. Therefore man's truest and fullest response to what is other than himself involves not only the manipulation of things, nor only the moral recognition of the claims of other persons, but also obedience to and co-operation with God. This response is the total response of his whole self to the totality of life. Because it is a response to God it will be a prayerful response, characterized by trust, hope, openness, courage, and joy. Within this total response man will now concentrate on thought, now on action, and now on prayer. The structure of his prayer will reflect the structure of his total response. Thus there will be moments of recollection and moments of aspiration; on the one hand thanksgiving, praise, and penitence, and on the other intercession and petition. These moments of prayer derive their validity from the total context within which they play their special roles. They are aspects of the approach of God to man and his world and the return of man with his world to God. Such I take to be the theological significance of prayer.

I will add one further thought and then I have done. Suspicious as I am of all questions which ask what is the use of prayer, I have no similar hesitation in asking what are the fruits of prayer. That there are fruits I do not doubt. Prayer does insinuate itself in the ongoing processes of the world. But the central question which we shall sooner or later find ourselves asking here is the question how we are to conceive God's activity in the world. The simplest answer to this question is that the love of God which is his activity penetrates into the world through our response to him. Our own actions possess a limited creativity, and as we open ourselves to the divine love so our own creativity is suffused with the creativity of God. Thus God's activity and man's receptivity are transmuted into a divine, human, natural activity. It all depends on us, and we depend on God. In praying for other people we open ourselves to God and make ourselves available to be used by him on their behalf in any way that may become possible. The ordinary way will be through our own ensuing actions. These may be very different from what they would have been had we not prayed, but not necessarily so. In any case we may intelligibly speak of God's working in us and through us. And perhaps we need not say any more. On the other hand the great causal nexus by which events in the world are connected may be more complex than we usually assume. For example, there may be parapsychological connexions as well as straightforward physical connexions. If this is so, what we do for others in response to the pressure of the divine love may be done not only in the physical actions which follow upon our prayers but also in the very acts of prayer. Whether this is so seems to me to be an open question. I myself am sufficiently agnostic not to rule the possibility out. Nor again should I rule out as impossible that God should in some way act apart from the natural nexus, that is, miraculously, although the mood of the present theological fashion, in which I confess I share (setting great store by our ever-increasing understanding of nature's own potentialities, and failing to discern any coherent pattern in what are alleged to be instances of God's miraculous activity), is to view this possibility with a large measure of reserve. Nevertheless, fruits of prayer there undoubtedly are; and we are called to pray, to respond to God with heart, mind, and spirit, not to fathom all the ways in which God uses our prayers for the furtherance of his purposes. "Look graciously upon us, Holy Spirit of God, and give us for our hallowing thoughts that pass into prayer, prayer that passes into love, love which is life indeed."